## MILNER CRAFT SERIES
# The Joy of
# Needlepoint

## DIANE WACHMAN

SALLY MILNER PUBLISHING

First published in 1994 by
Sally Milner Publishing Pty Ltd
558 Darling Street
Rozelle NSW 2039
Australia

© Diane Wachman, 1994

Design by Gatya Kelly, Doric Order
Colour photography by Andre Martin
Black and white photography and author's photo by
Benjamin Huie
Typeset in Australia by Doric Order
Printed in Australia by Impact Printing, Melbourne

National Library of Australia
Cataloguing-in-Publication data:

Wachman, Diane.
The Joy of Needlepoint.

ISBN 1 86351 124 5.

1. Canvas embroidery. 2. Canvas embroidery – Patterns.
I. Title. (Series: Milner craft series).

746.442

*The Joy of Needlepoint* is dedicated to Stanley – stitching
is as much a part of his life as it is mine.

## ACKNOWLEDGEMENTS

A big 'thank you ' goes out to those who helped me with stitching expertise, with comments and with encouragement. To Helen Collins, for reading my words over and over again. To Fay Taylor, for going through the book and using her writing knowledge for improvements. To Maralyn Hatch, Helen Collins and my sister, Maxine Benjamin, for giving me so much of their stitching time. My family and my friends, especially those at Mosman Needlecraft, have been so supportive – without interested family and friends, writing a book can be a lonely occupation. Thank you to Katrina Collins for the 'crafty' illustrations, to Janice St. Croix of Edgewater, Florida, USA for allowing me to use her colour wheel design, and to George of 'The Gainsborough Gallery', Manly, who puts so much care into framing my pieces.

# CONTENTS

# PREFACE

This book is for those of you who want to commence stitching as well as for those who want to gain extra knowledge in the craft I love. I still remember vividly needing a book that was going to guide me through the 'I wonder what I do now' stage, and, once I passed that stage, a book that would take me that bit further into stitches that would be more of a challenge. It seems that in one's stitching life there will always be 'I wonder what I do now' times, but the early fears recede and the quest for knowledge increases. The accumulation of my knowledge has spanned many years. Why couldn't this knowledge be passed on? And what better way to do this than in an easy-to-follow book; a book whose starting point is structured to suit that time when you decide you really would like to be able to do canvas work. You need to know about supplies, the dos and don'ts of stitching and the stitches themselves.

*The Joy of Needlepoint* is a reference stitch book that is easy to carry, easy to understand and presents easy designs to get you started. In addition, there are intermediate designs for a greater challenge. Yes, I know there have been many books on needlepoint over the years, but most of them included too many unwanted designs – it was the stitches I wanted to know about!

When I started I wanted a needlepoint work book. I wanted to learn not only the basic needlepoint stitch, but also a variety of not too complicated stitches that could enhance my chosen design. I knew that I would be working on canvas, but what size did I want to use? What fibres would be suitable for my chosen canvas? What different stitches could I use without too much difficulty?

This is the book of answers I am presenting here. It tells you about the materials and accessories you will need and includes well proven stitching hints. Its main purpose, however, is to provide you with a library of stitches in a form that is easy to use (and provide clear diagrams and brief explanations of their attributes and shortcomings). I hope my book proves an enjoyable guide to finding and employing different stitches. It has been written with the aim of passing on a delightful pastime that reaps rewarding results.

# CHAPTER 1

# THE SUBJECT OF NEEDLEPOINT

Before we start we need to discuss our subject a little. The first and most important thing, I feel, is the title that we have given the work we're doing. We call it Needlepoint. Many of you will have heard the term 'tapestry' and when you see what I am teaching you, I know you'll be saying, 'but that is tapestry'. Well, it really is *not*.

Tapestry is defined in the Oxford Dictionary as 'thick hand-woven textile fabric in which design is formed by weft stitches across parts of warp'. In other words, it is weaving. We are not weaving.

In an old book of mine our work is called 'needlepoint tapestry' meaning, I surmise, that it has a woven look about it, but is done with a needle. I often refer to it as 'canvas embroidery' as so many of the stitches we use can be done on even-weave material. If we delve even further and look up the French word for 'stitch', we find that it is 'point'. So, to my mind, that is what we are doing; we are stitching, on canvas with a needle. We are doing needlepoint. We are definitely not weaving!

The history of needlepoint dates from the 15th century, so even though we are not doing anything new, we're interpreting a craft that has been the source of happiness for many, many years. It's wonderful to know we are not letting such a joy fade into obscurity!

# CHAPTER 2

# CANVAS

Canvas is made mainly of linen or cotton, cotton being the most common in use today. There is also plastic canvas, which has its uses, but the size range is very limited.

Canvas has an even weave of open-mesh squares. Its size is dictated by the number of threads of canvas per 2.5 cm (1"). The more threads per 2.5 cm (1") the smaller the squares and the smaller the stitches formed on these squares. The finished design on a canvas with 18 threads per 2.5 cm (1") will be finer than the finished design on one with 12 threads per 2.5 cm (1").

For the different sizes of canvas I shall use the sign # meaning number, eg, a canvas with 12 threads per 2.5 cm (1") will be referred to as a #12 canvas.

It is important to use masking tape on the cut edges of your canvas. (See Masking Tape, page 8.)

There are two main types of canvas for needlepoint, penelope and mono, which have variations.

PENELOPE

This is used extensively in Europe, particularly for working large scenes and reproductions of Old Master paintings.

Penelope is a strong, double canvas where the threads are woven in pairs to create both large and small holes. For the most part, the large holes are used. But, such is the versatility of the canvas that when areas of fine detail, such as faces, are to be worked, the small and large holes are used. Remember, intricate detail cannot be reproduced by using only the large holes.

Penelope is also used when the design and colours to be worked are indicated on the canvas by tramming. What is tramming? Well, have you ever seen a canvas you thought was complete but which, on closer inspection, featured lines of wool on the front which were not secured firmly to the canvas underneath? That is tramming. It is placed on the canvas so that you can easily follow the design using your small tent-half cross stitch (Stitch No 35) – working over the top of the appropriate trammed line. Trammed canvases come in kit form containing everything you need to complete the design. Because many colours are used in these designs, they have been preselected for you and packaged in the kit to make the stitching of the trammed canvas a pleasure rather than a nightmare. Just so long as you choose a relatively simple trammed canvas, you'll find that this is an easy way of starting needlepoint.

MONO

This is a single canvas where the holes are uniform. These holes may be large or small depending on how many canvas threads are placed per 2.5 cm (1"). As mentioned previously, the more canvas threads there are per 2.5 cm (1") the smaller will be the holes. The most popular sizes for mono canvas are #10, #12, #14 and #18 which means 10, 12, 14 and 18 threads of canvas to 2.5 cm (1"). Mono canvas has movable warp and weft threads, the threads weaving over and under one another. This type of canvas is very strong and can be pulled and drawn, making it ideal for pulled and drawn thread work.

## MONO INTERLOCK

This does not have the strength of the regular mono canvas, but has other advantages. The threads are woven over and under one another but are 'locked'; that is, the strands are immovable. The most popular sizes for mono interlock canvas are #10, #12, #14 and #18. As a teacher, I find that for beginner students whose tension is likely to be rather irregular, the fact that the warp and weft are locked prevents their stitching from affecting the canvas. If a regular mono canvas is pulled too tight, the movable filaments of the canvas are pulled out of place. Mono interlock canvas does not pull out of shape as easily. As with all things, when one becomes more experienced in needlepoint, tension improves and there is less likelihood of exerting too much pressure on the canvas.

## CONGRESS CLOTH

This is an extremely fine cotton canvas usually of 24 threads per 2.5 cm (1"). It lends itself to designs with plenty of detail or to small geometric designs. The big plus with congress cloth is that you don't need to fill in the background – in fact, if the background were completely covered with stitches, the result would not be pleasing.

Canvas stitches can be worked on any even-weave base. I have done a piece on plastic fly-screen material and found it most successful!

   **Always** be generous with the amount of canvas you buy for your project. I allow 5 cm (2") on each side of my design area for a large piece of work. It is unnecessary to be so generous with a small design, but I still make an allowance so that, if the piece needs blocking, there will be sufficient canvas to hold on to in order to give a little tug to get it straight.

# CHAPTER 3

# FIBRES

## WOOL

Here I am referring to types of wool easily available in Australia. Needlepoint done with wool is still the most popular.

TAPESTRY WOOL

A 4 ply indivisible, smooth wool which is widely used for tent stitch, particularly on penelope canvas.

PERSIAN WOOL

A 3 ply divisible twisted wool.

APPLETON CREWEL WOOL

A thin wool used mostly for embroidery but suitable for canvas work. Because it is fine, it is possible to blend colours when using it on canvas that requires a number of strands.

DMC MEDICI WOOL

A thin wool used mostly for embroidery, but also successful in canvas work. Again, because it is fine, it's possible to blend colours when using it on canvas that requires a number of strands.

It is possible to use other types of wool for your work, remembering that those I have mentioned have greater durability for the specific demands of needlepoint.

For the new needlepoint stitcher, wool is probably the best fibre to use. Wool sounds simple enough, doesn't it? But, because there are many different types, the question of which wool is appropriate for the task needs addressing.

Let's first talk about the **basic** needlepoint stitch, tent stitch. There are three versions of this stitch: tent-continental, tent-basketweave and tent-half cross. (See pages 47, 48 and 50.) The wool we use is dictated by the size of canvas we are using. For example, if I am doing a piece in any of the basic tent stitches on #12 mono interlock canvas, I am able to use the regular 4 ply tapestry wool. This will cover the canvas and be comfortable to use. Persian wool can also be used but, because the three strands together are too thick, only two of the three strands will be required. If I tried to pull three strands of this wool through the canvas doing a diagonal stitch, it would be very difficult and I would end up with very sore fingers! Appleton crewel is much finer than Persian so I would need to use three strands on this size canvas. The same applies to DMC Medici. I must emphasise at this stage that I am talking about any one of the three versions of the basic tent stitch on a #12 mono interlock canvas.

## DYE LOTS AND QUANTITY OF FIBRE REQUIRED

If you are working a large area in one colour, it is extremely important to buy fibre all with the same dye lot number. It can be a disaster if you find you have not allowed enough fibre to complete, say, a background and, when you go to buy more, there is an obvious colour change due to the change in the dye lot. It is better to allow more than you think you will need rather than to run out.

A good way to work out your fibre requirements is to select a length of thread making it 45 cm (approx 18"). On the canvas you intend to use, we will say that this length of fibre stitched two 2.5 cm (1") squares. Work out how many 2.5 cm (1") squares are in the area you want to cover. Divide this by two and multiply this number by 45 cm (approx. 18"). Now you have the amount you are going to need. I would add 10 per cent to this figure just to be on the safe side. This method applies to all fibres.

## COTTONS

Again, I am referring to cottons easily available in Australia.

### PEARL COTTON

An indivisible softly twisted, shiny cotton. It comes in different sizes, the main sizes used in canvas work being Nos 3 and 5. No 3 is a thicker cotton than 5. However, smaller sizes are available and if a thin, shiny fibre is needed, it is worth looking at the other sizes, eg No 8.

Again I shall refer to the basic tent stitch done on a #12 mono interlock canvas. The No 3 Pearl Cotton covers this size of canvas very well. As the No 5 is a thinner cotton, it is used on a smaller canvas. (See Stitching Hint No 12 for the preparation of the skeins of Pearl Nos 3 and 5.)

### STRANDED COTTON

(Floss in USA terminology.) This is made up of separate fibres which can be pulled apart. Strands can be added or subtracted, depending on the thickness of the cotton required.

This time I shall refer to the basic tent stitch done on a #18 mono interlock canvas. Because it is a finer canvas, five strands of the stranded cotton will be needed to cover it with the basic tent stitch. It is important to strip this cotton. (See Notes with Reference to Strippable Fibres page 13.)

### BRODER COTTON OR SOFT EMBROIDERY COTTON

This is a flat, matt cotton which can be used in place of 4 ply tapestry wool on a #12 mono interlock canvas. It gives a much 'closer to the canvas' look because it is not as fluffy as the wool. It also comes in smaller sizes.

The examples of fibre coverage I have given feature the basic tent stitch, which is a **diagonal** stitch. The same fibre coverage applies to all the other diagonal stitches.

The **slanted**, **straight**, **crossed** and **combination** stitches may need a variation in the thickness of the fibre, (see Stitches, chapter 7).

There are many more types of fibre that can be used for canvas work, including silk, numerous synthetic threads and Brazilian embroidery threads. Metallic threads have their place in our work. Different size canvases use different sizes of metallic threads. Gold and silver thread can be used in conjunction with other fibres to achieve a particular effect.

It would be remiss of me not to mention the 'Watercolours' that have their own special place in canvas work, along with the overdyed wools and cottons. It is also possible to 'shade' your design with divisible fibres by mixing different coloured strands in your needle.

As soon as I have finished this book, I am quite sure other fibres will be on the market. When you feel confident with your stitching have a go and explore different applications with various fibres.

Whatever fibre you choose, it should be tried first on a small sample of the type of canvas you are intending to use. I never take for granted that the fibre I want to use will be the right one. I may find when I try it that it doesn't give the effect for which I'm striving. I may need more or fewer strands than I had originally thought. How much better it is to find this out first, before going too far, pretending the work looks good when I really know that it isn't right and that I must make alterations. PLEASE EXPERIMENT WITH YOUR CHOSEN FIBRE ON YOUR CHOSEN CANVAS TO MAKE SURE YOUR COVERAGE IS CORRECT.

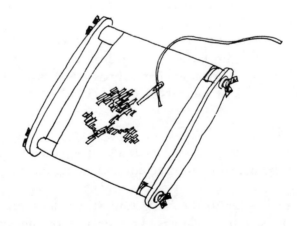

CHAPTER 4

# NEEDLES AND ACCESSORIES

## NEEDLES

We use tapestry needles for our work. That means they have a blunt end. The size of needle you require will be governed predominantly by the canvas size. You will soon know if your needle is too big. Your fingers will be complaining like mad that they can't get the needle through the canvas without a huge amount of pulling. Needlepoint is supposed to be relaxing and here you are extremely tense! Simply change to a size smaller needle. The main sizes of tapestry needle used range from No 18 to No 24. No 18 is suitable for canvas with large holes, eg #10 canvas. (A No 20 needle can also be used on this size of canvas.) The No 20 and the No 22 needles are probably the most versatile. On a #18 canvas, which is small, a No 22 is the most suitable. A No 22 or 24 can be used with congress cloth.

## ACCESSORIES

I shall run through the accessories alphabetically and mention whether or not I use them myself.

### CANVAS MARKERS

I use a water-erasable pen when I'm placing a design on canvas. Be aware of two factors. First, the outlines can fade if there is a lot of humidity in the air – understandable when you consider that the pen is designed expressly so that lines can be removed with water. Second, the lines can set if your work is exposed to heat. In spite of this, I find this type of marker quite suitable as I only need an impression of the design on my canvas.

The second method of marking canvas utilises a pen designed specifically as a canvas marker. It doesn't bleed, but you must remember that once the lines are on your canvas they are there for good. Many times, this permanency is what you want.

**Never** use a biro. You know how they can smudge on paper – imagine what they do when water is used to block your stitched piece. I have seen what can happen when a biro has been used under the stitching and the piece has needed to be blocked. The ink bleeds through the stitching and the result is heart breaking – don't let that happen to you. I avoid using a pencil because I find the graphite can come off on a light-coloured fibre. However, if I found it necessary, I would use the hardest pencil I could find.

### FRAMES

The use of a working frame is another highly personal thing. I am what could only be called a distorter, so I need a frame unless I am working on an extremely small piece. I mostly work on a roller frame where the work is attached to the webbing on the two rods with extremely strong running stitches. I make sure that the beginning and end of the running stitch is reinforced. The rods, which come in a variety of lengths, are then slotted into the side pieces and secured with the wing nut. Just a tip – make sure that when you put the side pieces onto the rollers, you put wood to wood and then add the washer and, finally, the wing nut. The work can be rolled either up or down in order that your piece is where you want it to be for stitching.

If necessary, you can lace each side of your canvas to the side pieces of your frame once your work is in position on the frame. This is achieved simply by attaching firmly to the side of the canvas and going around the side pieces, then back to the canvas, back around the side pieces, and so on. I admit it is a bit of a nuisance when you want to roll your canvas and you have to undo and then redo your lacing, but it is better than having your lovely piece of work distorted.

Also available are floor frames which comprise a roller frame on legs for greater ease when stitching a large piece. (I have a husband who makes me small stretcher frames if I need it. Lucky, aren't I?) Don't let anyone tell you canvas can be worked in a hoop. Trying to force it into one will be extremely damaging for the canvas and will ruin the stitching where it is wedged under the edge of the hoop. To my mind, it is a complete no-no.

LAYING TOOL

This is used when you are working with strippable fibres, eg silk and stranded cotton. (See Notes with Reference to Strippable Fibres, page 13.) A laying tool comes in many forms, but, basically, it is a fat, blunt needle which you hold in your non-stitching hand and over which your strands of fibre are smoothly laid as they go down into the canvas. The laying tool is pulled out just before the fibre comes into contact with the canvas.

LIGHTING

As you can well imagine, good light is essential for our work. As a right-handed stitcher, I find that my canvas is seen at its best if the light comes from my left side. Then, there is no worry of my working arm obstructing the light. At night-time, I have a double spotlight on a stand by the left side of my chair and the light shines directly onto my work. There are also lights available with magnifiers which may suit your needs.

MASKING TAPE

This is a very important accessory as, frequently, the canvas you want to stitch is bare. Therefore, if it is penelope or mono canvas, it will fray. If it is a mono interlock canvas, the sharp edges will catch the fibre you are using and you will slowly be driven mad. You need a 2.5 cm (1") wide tape. Make sure it is the best you can buy. There can be problems with it as humidity causes it to lift off and become very sticky. All you can do is replace the tape if this happens. I have also tried a 3M Micro tape used by doctors and have found it most reliable. You can buy it at chemist shops. If you don't want to use tape, stitch bias binding around your canvas or turn a hem and machine it. I'm not interested in all that, so I have had many happy years with masking tape!

## NEEDLE CASE
A needle case is such a personal thing. I have one made for me by a friend and I use it all the time. It is lovely because every time I use it I think of her with happy memories. It is better to place your needles in flannelette rather than in felt. (Needles will rust after a certain time if left in felt. Possibly this is dictated by your climatic conditions.)

## NEEDLE MAGNET
Any magnet is useful for holding needles in one place. They are sometimes sold on a pin which can be attached to your clothing or to your work bag. I have also seen them on a needle case. You'll no doubt use your magnet according to your needs. I have recently discovered a box that has magnets inside it so your needles sit where you put them – they don't even bounce around!

## NEEDLE THREADER
A must for every stitcher. I don't go anywhere without mine. The threader you need is stronger than that used for ordinary sewing cotton. It has a metal eye on each end, one larger than the other. The chosen eye of your needle threader is put through the eye of your needle and, because of its size, it is a simple matter to put your fibre through this metal eye and then pull the needle threader back through the eye of your own needle. It is especially useful when you are using Pearl cotton. A tip here; it is a good idea to place a piece of wool through the small hole in the centre of your threader so that you can keep track of it. There have been times when the little devil manages to lose itself in the bottom of my bag!

## THIMBLE
I have never been a thimble person, but I realise that there are many people who wouldn't stitch unless they could use one. Because our stitching is done with a blunt needle, a thimble is needed less than it would be if we were using a sharp one.

## THIMBLETTE
I have found a thimblette extremely useful over the years. It's simply a rubber finger-covering with small raised bumps, it's main purpose being to separate pieces of paper for counting. When a fibre I want to use is a little tight to pull through the canvas, a thimblette saves wear and tear on my fingers. You can buy them at stationery shops and newsagents.

## SCISSORS
I use two different types of scissors. First, I have a large pair that I use for cutting canvas. They can be the type you use for cutting paper. You're cutting a tough

material remember, so you would not use that 'special' pair you keep for cutting fabric. Second, I have small scissors with pointy ends – I stress here that they need to be sharp. Nothing is worse than sawing away at a piece of fibre when all it really needs is a quick nick with a nice sharp pair of scissors.

Nail scissors do a very good job. They also are great for ripping out. Errors are not the prerogative of the beginner; every stitcher makes them. The curved blades will easily go under the stitches that somehow or other have ended up in the wrong place! I stress here, please be careful how you cut – **don't** cut the canvas.

TWEEZERS

If I am using my curved-blade scissors and am cutting out a section, I shall have little cut ends all over the place. This is when my trusty tweezers come into play. I couldn't do without them. They make the whole unfortunate exercise a lot easier.

## DESIGN HINTS

My idea here is to pass on a few hints rather than to write an essay on the subject of design. Many people have a natural design ability, but for those of us who don't, there are many ways to become more creative. The basis of your design could come from numerous sources, including photographs, postcards or even the drawings found in colouring books. The latter can be traced onto the canvas with a water-erasable pen or a canvas marking pen. (Both pens are discussed in detail in this chapter.) A photocopier that enlarges and reduces is a great help if your chosen design is smaller or larger than required. Remember, your choice of design should not be too detailed or the areas to be worked too small; these factors will limit the range of stitches you can use.

I know it can be quite alarming when you have either placed your design on your piece of canvas, or bought a canvas with a design on it, and it is staring at you, waiting for you to begin. Isolate an area on which to commence, then refer to this book and look through the stitches. Choose a stitch you like, then choose a fibre and experiment either on the edge of your work, or on a practice piece of canvas the same count as your working canvas. You're ready to take the plunge and begin your work! You will find that once that first stitch is placed, ideas will flow from there – just go for it.

# CHAPTER 5
# STITCHING HINTS

These are all tried and true for me. Do read them through before you commence stitching and refer back to them as often as necessary.

1   If your skein of wool or cotton has a drawing of hands on the label, pull the fibre in the direction indicated by the hands.

2   Your working fibre must not be too long. Approximately 45 cm (18") is the correct length. A quick method of measuring is to hold the fibre in your hand and pull the rest of the skein down to a little below your elbow. Cut at this point. The thread can be longer when you are doing straight stitches, but don't get carried away and have it so long that you need your arm to be twice as long to pull the fibre through in one go. Also, the thread can become frayed and worn by repeated pulling through the canvas.

3   Whenever possible, come up with your needle in an empty hole and go down into a hole that is already occupied. (This is not always possible.)

4   When wanting to stitch the same colour in a different area on your design, don't 'jump' with your fibre across the back for more than 2.5 cm (1").

5   Do not pull your stitches too tight.

6   Do not draw on your canvas with a biro or with a soft pencil. Use only a needlepoint marker or a water-erasable pen.

7   If you are using two colours or more and you don't want to keep threading and re-threading, use more than one needle. If you do this, make sure you bring the needle you are **not** using to the front of your work and anchor it a distance away from your present stitching. If you leave it hanging at the back, there will be a tangled, unhappy mess of fibres.

8   Don't leave your needle threaded into your work if the atmosphere is humid. I had a disaster in far north Queensland with a nasty rust mark on my white canvas. The needle had been in the canvas for only one day!

9   It is possible to paint canvas with acrylic paint. For example, you want a dark background and as you are about to start you can see that the white canvas is going to 'smile' through the covering fibre where you don't want it. Get some acrylic paint and paint the canvas the same colour as the dark fibre. Don't saturate the canvas, use just sufficient to do the job. (I had to paint over my rust mark with white acrylic paint.)

10  When counting your threads of canvas, especially when there are many of them, lay your canvas on a firm base, take your needle and run it firmly over the threads. There will be a click as you go over each thread. This way you not only see the threads, but can also hear the number you are counting.

11 When using a white fibre of some kind, always stitch it first. I can hear you saying – 'But it will get dirty'. The reason for working it first is that, if you have a dark colour next to where you intend to stitch with white, every time you bring the white through the hole with the dark colour in it, you will find the white picks up some of the tiny fibres from the dark colour. Your lovely white is no longer a lovely white.

12 When using the Pearl cotton skeins Nos 3 and 5, I take the wrappers off and cut the cotton at the knot. Then I thread the number onto the skein. I halve the skein leaving the number at the top. Then I place the skein around someone's finger, or whatever else is handy, and proceed to plait it loosely putting a little tie at the bottom of the plait. This way my skein is then neat and ready to use at any time – and I know the number. When I pull a piece out, I cut it in half because cotton loses its lustre very easily when pulled repeatedly in and out of the canvas. The friction of canvas is not kind to the cotton.

13 You can start your work with a waste knot. This knot in your working fibre is placed on the front of your work at least 5 cm (2") ahead of where your stitching goes. You should train yourself to keep this waste knot as much as possible horizontal or vertical to the commencement of your stitching. The tail at the back formed by the waste knot is secured as you stitch. The knot can be cut off when the stitches have been worked up to it. Pull it firmly before you cut so that the thread springs to the back of the canvas and is hidden in the existing stitches. Once you have sufficient wool on your canvas, you can, if you wish, join in a new thread by running it along the back for approximately 5 cm (2") and add a small backstitch for extra strength.

14 Finish off your working fibre by running in for 5 cm (2") on the back of your work. If you feel that extra security is needed, put in a small backstitch. When running along at the back for any reason, do not dig your needle too far in as this may alter the tension on the front of your work.

15 When you want to work a straight stitch and there is very little backing, simply weave the fibre in and out of a few threads of the blank canvas, selecting an area that will be covered eventually with stitching. To finish off straight stitching, weave your wool in at the back for 5 cm (2") and make a backstitch before cutting off the end.

16 When you have a straight stitch meeting a diagonal or slanted one, they must share the same holes. If not, you'll find that a thread of canvas shows at the point at which the two meet.

17 If you find your fibre is twisting as you stitch, take your needle and run it down your fibre as far as the canvas, then back to its stitching position. This takes the twist out of the fibre. You will need to do this regularly.

18 When stitching your pattern, fill in as many complete stitches as you can in the space you have on your design. When the edge of the design area is reached, you very often find you cannot put in a whole stitch. Put in as much of the stitch as is possible, making sure you keep the sense of the pattern. This 'part' stitch is known as a 'compensatory stitch'. (See Glossary of Terms, Compensatory Stitches, page 109.)

19 There are two important definitions to be memorised:
   a) the strands making up your canvas are referred to as **threads**.
   b) the intersection where the threads of the canvas cross one another are referred to as **mesh**.

I shall be referring to **threads** and **mesh** in the stitch diagrams.

### NOTES WITH REFERENCE TO STRIPPABLE FIBRES

- When using plied fibres, eg wool and cotton, it should be 'stripped'. This is to ensure smoothness and better coverage with your stitching. You strip the strands apart and put back together the number required. There is a very simple method of doing this. Take your cut piece of thread and, holding it in one hand with the cut edge pointing upwards, individually pull out each strand. As you pull each one out, smooth the remaining strands down with your free hand and then repeat the process until you have the required number of strands.

- Wool has a 'nap'. When you rub your fingers along the strand of wool, the hair fibres stand up, favouring one direction more than the other. Another way of discovering which way the fibres lie is to run the strand of wool along your top lip. ( I have been known to have a good sneeze after doing this.) The end to thread is the one that has the flattest hair fibres. I stress here for beginners not to be put off if you find it difficult to see the way the fibres are lying. I am making a fine point which becomes easier to discover as you become a more experienced stitcher.

N.B. The number of plies of fibre required will vary according to the size of the canvas you are covering.

- An extension on the above information is when you are using a synthetic fibre, such as Marlitt or its equivalent, which has a very definite mind of its own. The fibre should be dampened before use. One of my students kept a dampened Chux in a plastic bag and ran the fibre through this cloth which gave sufficient amount of dampness to make it workable. Another swore by her cosmetic sponge – used only for the thread, of course. In one class, we immersed the Marlitt in a glass of water and, after we took it out and left it to dry, it behaved beautifully.

Finally, do remember to experiment with stitches and with fibres that you want to use. The best place to do this is either at the bottom, or the side of the canvas on which you are working, so that you are using the same canvas for practising as for your actual piece.

# CHAPTER 6

# STITCH FAMILIES, STITCH IMPACT AND STITCH KEYS

We now get down to what you have all been waiting for – the stitches themselves. And, before we go any further, I should explain that I am going to use the names for the stitches that I have learnt over the years. I do realise that many have more than one name and I have noticed that they sometimes vary between the UK and the USA. The stitches I am presenting here are the ones I have found the most useful. If I had included all the canvas work stitches this book would be difficult to lift!

The stitches have been divided into 'families' and each family will have a short explanation on the basic 'ingredients' of the family.

## DIAGONAL AND SLANTED FAMILY

Probably the most used of all the families is the **diagonal** one. The family name is the key to the shape of the stitch. Each or every part of this stitch is on the diagonal, or the 45° angle. The stitch itself may cover any number of mesh (see Stitching Hints 19b), but **always remains at this angle**. The **slanted** family is made up of stitches which are not on the 45° angle, but which are at a slant in some direction. As this slanted family have a lesser angle, they tend to have parts that are more closely grouped.

## STRAIGHT FAMILY

All stitch parts in this family are straight, whether they are on the horizontal or the vertical. They generally require a **thickening** of the usable fibre in order to cover the canvas sufficiently. In order not to have canvas showing, straight stitches need to share the holes used by, for example, the diagonal stitches. This shared straight stitch needs to be pulled firmly; otherwise, it will overwhelm the sharing smaller stitch. The holes may be a little crowded, but the overall appearance is much improved.

## CROSSED AND COMBINATION FAMILY

First the **crossed** family. A longer length of fibre is needed to complete each stitch, so make sure you allow a sufficient number of skeins for your required stitching. Many of the crossed family stitches stand away from the surface of the canvas. Crossed stitches, on the whole, do not give good covering on the back of the canvas. This can affect durability. The **combination** family comprises stitches with a mixture of diagonal, slanted, straight and crossed – in any combination. They are generally a little more complicated and I would suggest that they are used when you feel comfortable with the more straightforward stitches in the other families.

There are two keys listed here for you to study before you look at the diagrams.

### FIRST KEY – THE STITCH DIAGRAMS

The direction of the stitch is indicated with arrows. The stitch comes up through the canvas where the number or letter is placed and goes down through the canvas at the tip of the arrow.

The first row is in black     ↑ = first row

The second row is in grey     ↑ = second row

When the letters are upside down, the canvas is to be turned upside down. **When doing the stitches, follow the direction of the arrows.**

### SECOND KEY – THE EXPLANATION FOR STITCH IMPACT

Here, we are talking about the impact a stitch makes visually. I have divided the key into three general categories: light, medium and heavy. A different emphasis in your work will call for different stitch impacts. Sometimes you'll want a stitch to dominate. In this case, look for a heavy impact stitch. When doing a background stitch, you may want it to be unobtrusive, so a light impact stitch is what you're after.

Impact can alter not only with the individual stitch structure, but also with the fibres you choose. The composition of the fibres goes from smooth to rough and from matt to shiny. Your eye will guide you as to which fibre will help create the effect you are trying to achieve. Do experiment before making a final decision. As you do more stitching, you'll be able to see quite quickly whether the stitch and the fibre you have chosen make the desired impact.

# CHAPTER 7

# STITCHES

## DIAGONAL AND SLANTED FAMILY
### *Byzantine*

### STITCH NO 1
### STITCH IMPACT – MEDIUM

The size of the stitch can vary by increasing the number of mesh covered. The steps can be wider or narrower by varying the number of parts to each step. If you wanted longer steps you would continue across further and down further. Good for countryside, such as hills, and for backgrounds.

**Technique:** Each part of this stitch is over two mesh on the diagonal. There are four parts to each of the step-like formation. (4) becomes the first part of the downward step. The 2nd row (a, b, c, d etc.) is also over two mesh on the diagonal and fits into the previous row. The rows continue in this way. The stitch can be worked up or down the canvas.

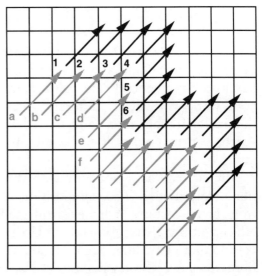

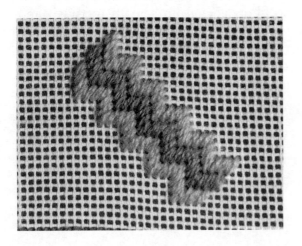

# *Cashmere*

STITCH NO 2

STITCH IMPACT – LIGHT

Cashmere forms rectangular units. Good for background. Interesting checkerboard effect when two colours are used. Distorts the canvas so should be worked on a working frame.

**Technique:** This stitch is worked diagonally across the canvas in units. (1) is over one mesh, (2) commences directly below it and over two mesh, (3) directly below again and still over two mesh, (4) placed to the right of (3) and over one mesh. There is then a skip hole on the diagonal and the whole unit is repeated (5, 6 etc.) In the 2nd row (a) meets (4), (b) fills the skip hole (c) meets (5) and (d) meets (6). Small rectangles are formed that sit below or above one another. Can be worked down and up the canvas.

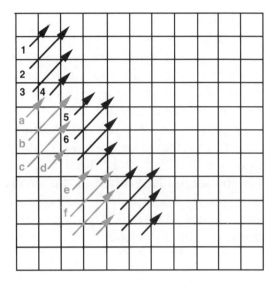

# Cashmere-continuous

STITCH NO 3

STITCH IMPACT – LIGHT

Has a nice flow to it, but it does distort the canvas. It is easier for compensating than the other cashmeres. Useful in many designs as it fits into small areas. Can be a good background stitch – but **beware** of distortion.

**Technique:** This is a continuous cashmere stitch. (1) is over one mesh, (2) is directly below (1) and over two mesh, (3) is directly below (2) and still over two mesh, (4) is to the right of (3) and over one mesh, (5) is directly below (4) and over two mesh. The correct cashmere-continuous sequence continues. In the 2nd row, the first short stitch (a) meets (3) the second long stitch of the 1st row. The row then continues in the cashmere-continuous sequence. Can be worked down and up the canvas.

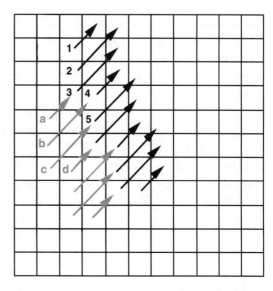

# Cashmere-framed continuous

### STITCH NO 4
### STITCH IMPACT – LIGHT

The stitch is given dimension by the row of tent stitch that is between each cashmere-continuous row. It looks lovely as a background stitch and stunning with the use of two colours. It does distort so would be better worked on a working frame.

**Technique:** This is a cashmere-continuous stitch framed with a tent stitch. (1) is over one mesh. (2) is directly below (1) and over two mesh. (3) is directly below (2) and over two mesh. (4) is to the right of (3) and over one mesh. The sequence continues. The 2nd row is a tent stitch that follows the line set by the cashmere-continuous sequence. The 3rd row is the cashmere-continuous stitch fitting next to the tent stitch. The following row will be a tent row and the rows alternate in this way.

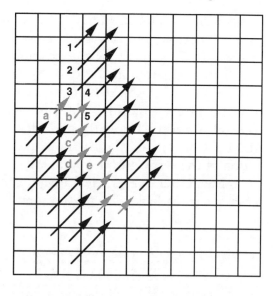

# Cashmere-horizontal

## STITCH NO 5
## STITCH IMPACT – LIGHT

In some instances it will be more convenient to work the cashmere units in this way. You may want a horizontal border. Distortion of the canvas can occur if you are doing a large area – use a working frame.

**Technique:** The cashmere units are worked next to one another across the canvas. (1, 2, 3, 4) show the position of the first cashmere unit. (5, 6, 7, 8) show the position of the next unit. In the 2nd row (a) meets (6), (b) is directly below (a), (c) is directly below (b) and (d) is to the right of (c). (e, f, g, h) show the position of the next unit. The units fit next to one another across the canvas. Each cashmere unit looks exactly the same.

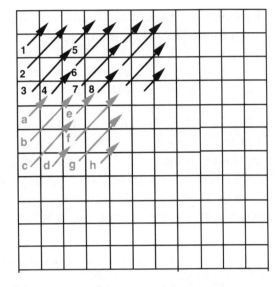

# *Cashmere-vertical*

STITCH NO 6
STITCH IMPACT – LIGHT

In some instances, it will be more convenient to work the cashmere units in this way. You may want a vertical border. Distortion can occur, so if you are doing a large area, use a working frame.

**Technique:** The cashmere units are worked vertically down the canvas. (1, 2, 3, 4) show the position of the first cashmere unit. (5, 6, 7, 8) show the position of the next unit below the first one. In the 2nd row (a) meets (3), (b) is directly below (a), (c) is directly below (b) and (d) is to the right of (c). (e, f, g, h) show the position of the next unit. The units fit next to one another going down the canvas. Each cashmere unit looks exactly the same.

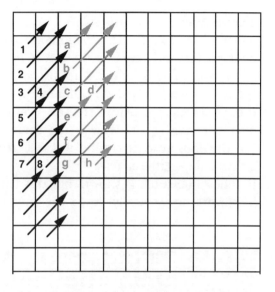

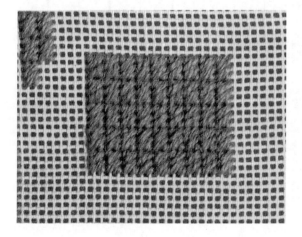

# Gobelin-diagonal

## STITCH NO 7
## STITCH IMPACT – LIGHT

This stitch forms horizontal and vertical rows and can be used to depict any type of horizontal or vertical line. It can be made larger and often is when a wider line is required for a particular design, or for a wider divisional line.

**Technique:** A. (1) This stitch is over two mesh of canvas on the diagonal. (2) is next to (1) and remains over two mesh of canvas. The stitch continues in this way. The 2nd row (a) commences two threads of canvas below (1) and again is over two mesh. Each row is the same as the previous row. It can be worked from either side of the canvas.

B. The same stitch is shown, but this time it is working vertically down the canvas.

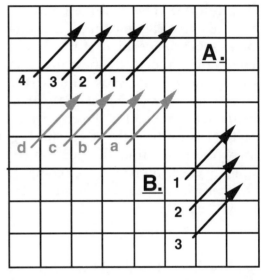

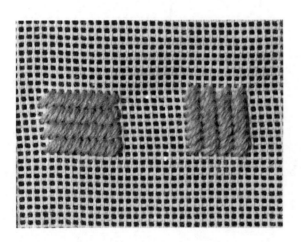

# Gobelin-slanted

STITCH NO 8
STITCH IMPACT – LIGHT

Not as tight as gobelin-slanted (interlock 2x1) and works very well when a horizontal look is required. eg good when fence railings are being stitched.

**Technique:** This is a slanted stitch. (1) goes up two threads of canvas and across one. (2) is right next to (1) and exactly the same. The stitch continues in this way. In the 2nd row (a) is started two threads below (1) and is up two threads of canvas and across one thread. (b) is directly next to (a) and so on. The stitch can be worked from either side of the canvas.

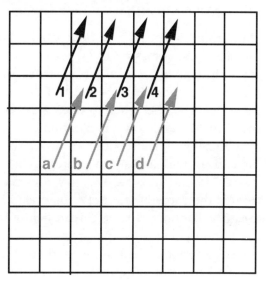

# Gobelin-slanted (interlock 2x1)

STITCH NO 9

STITCH IMPACT – LIGHT

This is the tightest of the gobelin interlocking stitches. It is useful in an area requiring a compact look, being an extremely flat stitch. Your fibre may need to be thinner for this stitch.

**Technique:** This is a slanted stitch. The needle stitch comes up at (1) goes up over two threads of canvas and across one thread of canvas. (2) is started in the hole next to (1). The stitch proceeds in this way. In the 2nd row (a) commences one thread below (1). It is up over two threads of canvas and across one thread. (b) is placed in the hole next to (a) etc. Each row is the same as the previous one. The 3rd row commences one thread below (a) and interlocks with the first row. The fourth interlocks with the second etc. Can be worked from either side of the canvas.

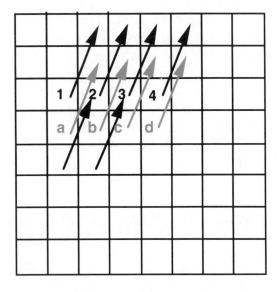

# *Gobelin-slanted (interlock 4x2)*

STITCH NO 10
STITCH IMPACT – MEDIUM

This is a tight stitch due to the locking but its size creates a medium impact stitch. Good for long-trunked trees. The stitch can be larger by making it two threads taller, but watch for snagging.

**Technique:** This is a slanted stitch. The needle comes up at (1), goes up over four threads of canvas and across two threads of canvas. (2) commences in the hole next to (1), (3) is next to (2) etc. In the 2nd row (a) commences two threads below (1). It is up four threads of canvas and across two threads of canvas. (b) is placed in the hole next to (a) etc. Each row is the same as the previous one. The 3rd row commences two threads below (a) and interlocks with the 1st row, the fourth interlocks with the 2nd etc. Can be worked from either side of the canvas.

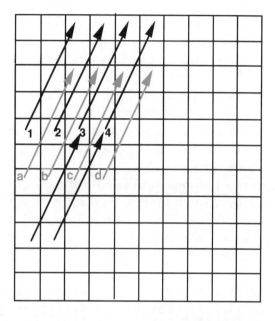

# *Jacquard*

STITCH NO 11

STITCH IMPACT – LIGHT

This is the smallest of the jacquards. It can be made larger by increasing the mesh covered by the Byzantine part of the stitch. A good background stitch worked in one colour. Creates movement which looks effective in trees, for example.

**Technique:** The first part of this stitch is a Byzantine stitch which covers two mesh (1) and continues across the canvas to the right for four parts of the step-like formation (2, 3, 4). (4) becomes the first part of the downward steps and works down the canvas for a total of four units (4, 5, 6, 7). It goes across for four parts of the step and down again. It proceeds in this fashion. In the 2nd row (a, b etc.) is a tent stitch and fits in directly next to the first row. This tent stitch forms a divider between the rows of Byzantine.

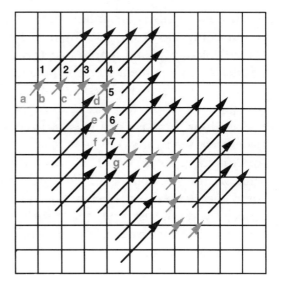

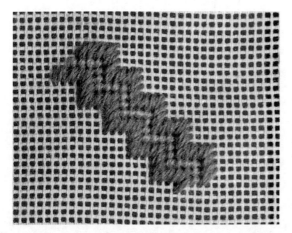

# *Kalem*

STITCH NO 12

STITCH IMPACT – LIGHT

This stitch is small and is used mostly in small areas. It creates fine lines which look like knitting. At times I have used it to create a roof, small buildings, tails of birds and fence posts. Quite a different look is achieved by alternating two colours.

**Technique:** (1) is up two threads and across one thread. (2) comes up directly below (1) and is the same as (1). The stitches follow in this way. (5) shows how the two halves of the stitch come together. (6) follows (5) etc. A small v is created with this stitch. In the 2nd row (a) commences two threads across from (5) and joins up with the top of (5). (d) creates the other half of the stitch with (a) and the v is formed. Each v row sits next to the previous one.

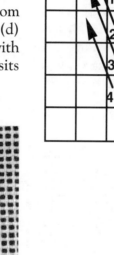

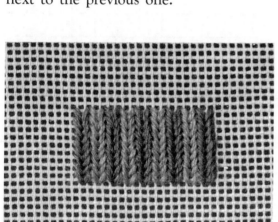

# Knotted stitch

STITCH NO 13

STITCH IMPACT – LIGHT

This is a nice neat stitch which will not need thick fibre. It has a light effect and can be used in small areas. Suitable for use in most designs.

**Technique:** (1) is up over three threads and across one thread. (2) crosses the middle of (1). (3) is next to (1) and (4) crosses the middle of (3). The stitch proceeds across the canvas in this way. In the 2nd row (a) comes up two threads down from (1) and goes up over three threads and across one thread to meet (2). (b) crosses (a). (c) is next to (a) and meets (4). (d) crosses (c). The 3rd row commences two threads down from (a) and follows the set pattern. Each row follows as the one before. Can be worked from either side of the canvas.

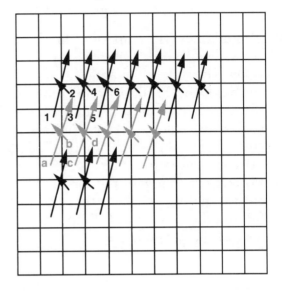

# Milanese

## STITCH NO 14
## STITCH IMPACT – MEDIUM

When this is stitched, it has the look of arrows going in two different directions. It makes a good-looking background stitch because it has such a pleasing flow.

**Technique:** In the 1st row (1) is over one mesh, (2) directly below it and over two mesh, (3) directly below and over three mesh, (4) directly below and over four mesh. (5) is two threads across and one thread up from (4) and begins the whole unit again. The 2nd row fits into the first row. (a) the largest part of the unit meets (1) the smallest part of the first unit, (b) meets (2), (c) meets (3) and (d) the smallest part of the unit meets (4) the largest part of the first unit. (e) begins the whole unit again. They proceed in this manner. Can be worked down and up the canvas.

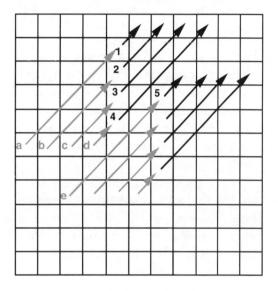

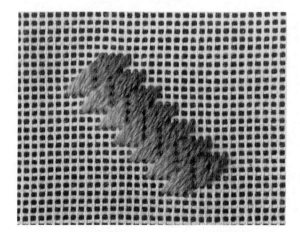

# Moorish

## STITCH NO 15
### STITCH IMPACT – LIGHT

This is one of my favourite stitches and I nearly always find a place for it in my piece. It resembles stairs. The tent dividing the rows of scotch-continuous give it dimension. Good for landscapes, roof tops and, in one colour, very good for backgrounds.

**Technique:** This is a scotch-continuous stitch framed with a tent stitch. (1) is over one mesh. (2) is directly below (1) and over two mesh. (3) is directly below (2) and over three mesh. (4 and 5) are to the right of (3) and over two and one mesh. The sequence continues. The 2nd row is a tent stitch that follows the line set by the scotch-continuous sequence. The 3rd row is the scotch-continuous stitch fitting next to the tent stitch. The following row will be a tent row and the rows alternate in this way.

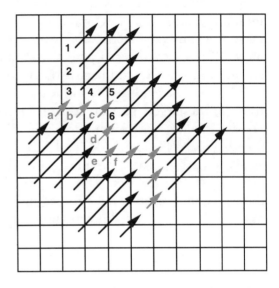

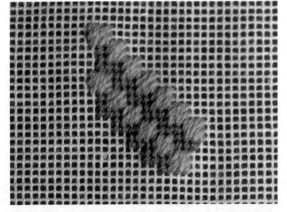

# Mosaic

STITCH NO 16
STITCH IMPACT – LIGHT

Probably the most useful of all the small stitches. Good for background, especially when worked in one colour. Two colours give a whole new look to the stitch. Very good for small areas. Distorts the canvas so should be worked on a working frame.

**Technique:** This is the basic mosaic unit formed by three different movements. (1) over one mesh, (2) commenced directly below it and over two mesh, (3) to the right and over one mesh. There is then a skip hole on the diagonal and the unit is repeated (4, 5, 6). These units continue diagonally down the canvas. In the 2nd row (a) meets (3), (b) fills the skip hole and (c) meets (4). There is then a skip hole and the unit is repeated. Little square boxes are formed that sit below or above one another. Can be worked down and up the canvas.

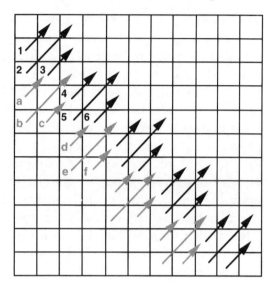

# *Mosaic-continuous*

STITCH NO 17
STITCH IMPACT – LIGHT

A useful stitch, good for small areas. Distorts the canvas so should be worked on a working frame. It is easier for compensating than the other mosaics. The stitch can be made larger by going over two and three mesh instead of one and two.

**Technique:** This is a continuous mosaic stitch with no gaps between the mosaic units. (1) is over one mesh, (2) is directly below (1) and over two mesh, (3) is to the right of (2) and over one mesh. (4) is below and over two mesh, (5) is to the right and over one mesh etc. The stitch proceeds in a diagonal direction. In the 2nd row (a) the two mesh stitch meets (1) the one mesh stitch of the 1st row and (b) the one mesh stitch meets (2) the two mesh stitch of the 1st row etc. The stitch proceeds like this in a diagonal direction. Can be worked down and up the canvas.

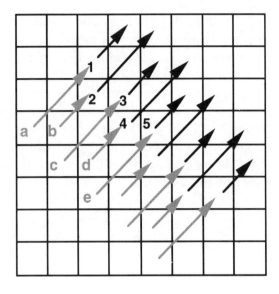

# *Mosaic-horizontal*

### STITCH NO 18
### STITCH IMPACT – LIGHT

In some instances it will be more convenient to work the mosaic units in this way, especially if you want to have a horizontal line of the stitch or create a horizontal border. Distorts the canvas so should be worked on a working frame.

**Technique:** The mosaic units are worked next to one another horizontally across the canvas. (1, 2, 3) show the position of the first unit, (4, 5, 6) show the next unit. In the 2nd row the small stitch (a) meets (3) the small stitch on the 1st row. The large stitch (b) meets (5) the large stitch on the 1st row. (c) is directly below (b). (d, e, f) show the next unit. The units fit alongside one another across the canvas.

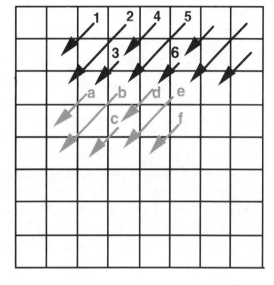

# Mosaic-reverse

### STITCH NO 19
### STITCH IMPACT – LIGHT

Single hole gaps are formed with 'mosaic-reverse' and give a lighter look to the stitch. Distortion is kept to a minimum as the different stitch directions of the unit pull against one another. A good background stitch.

**Technique:** This is the basic mosaic unit. In the 1st row (1) is over one mesh, (2) is directly below and over two mesh, (3) to the right and over one mesh. There is then a skip hole on the diagonal and the unit is repeated. These units continue diagonally down the canvas. In the 2nd row (a, b, c) is the basic mosaic unit worked in the opposite direction. (a) is begun four threads across from (1). There is a skip hole between each unit. These units continue diagonally down the canvas. When you are comfortable with the stitching, it can be done down or up the canvas.

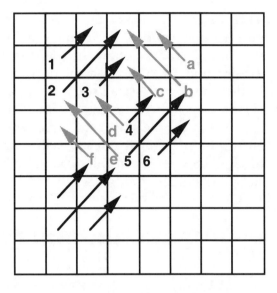

# *Mosaic-vertical*

STITCH NO 20
STITCH IMPACT – LIGHT

In some instances, it will be more convenient to work the mosaic units in this way, especially if you want to have a vertical line of the stitch or create a vertical border. Distorts the canvas so should be worked on a working frame.

**Technique:** The mosaic units are worked vertically down the canvas. (1, 2, 3) show the position of the first mosaic unit. The second unit (4, 5, 6) is placed directly below the first unit. The units proceed vertically down the canvas. In the 2nd row (a) meets (3) (b) meets (5) and (c) is to the right of (b). (d, e, f) show the position of the next unit. The units proceed vertically down the canvas.

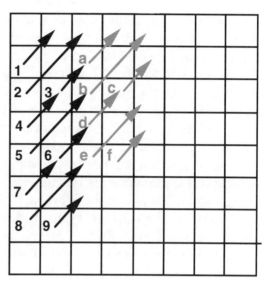

# Mosaic checker

STITCH NO 21

STITCH IMPACT – LIGHT

An interesting variation to both mosaic and tent. It gives a two-dimensional effect and is suitable for small design areas. Wonderful in two colours. I have worked it as a background to a tiny Christmas stocking – it looks good!

**Technique:** This is the basic mosaic unit with four tent-continental stitches worked between each unit. (1) is over one mesh (2) is directly below (1) and over two mesh (3) is to the right of (2) and over one mesh. (4, 5, 6, 7) are the four tent-continental stitches. (8) commences the mosaic unit again. In the 2nd row the four tent stitches are under the mosaic unit and the mosaic units are under the four tent stitches. Can be worked from either side of the canvas. When working from the right side of the canvas the mosaic sequence can be (3, 2, 1) followed by the tent-continental stitches.

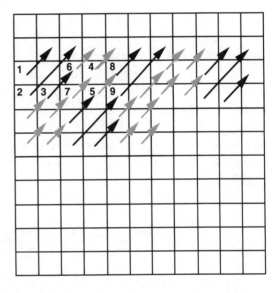

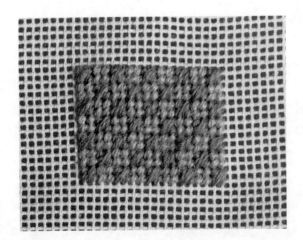

# *Nubuko*

STITCH NO 22
STITCH IMPACT – LIGHT

A very pleasant stitch that blends nicely into any piece. Particularly good for skies when it is possible to blend colours.

**Technique:** The first part of this stitch is over 1 mesh (1). (2) is begun directly below (1) and is over 3 mesh. (3) is across two threads and up one from (2). It is over one mesh. (4) is below (3) and is over three mesh. The stitch proceeds in this way. In the 2nd row (a) the three mesh part of the stitch meets (7) the one mesh part of the stitch from the 1st row. The one mesh part of the 2nd row (b) meets (6) the three mesh part of the 1st row. This continues in all the ensuing rows. Can be worked in either direction.

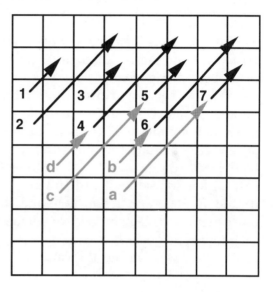

# *Scotch*

STITCH NO 23
STITCH IMPACT – MEDIUM

A good stitch for background, but it does distort the canvas. Should be worked on a working frame.The scotch units can be made larger, always having an uneven number of parts. Be careful as it gets larger that it does not snag.

**Technique:** This is the basic scotch unit. (1) is over one mesh, (2) commenced directly below it is over two mesh, (3) directly below again and over three mesh, (4 and 5) move to the right over two mesh and one mesh. There is a skip hole on the diagonal and the unit is repeated. In the 2nd row (a) meets (4), (b) meets (5), (c) fills the skip hole, (d and e) meet (6 and 7). There is a skip hole and the unit is repeated. When they are stitched, each unit is a square box. Can be worked diagonally down and up the canvas.

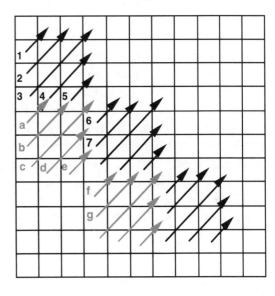

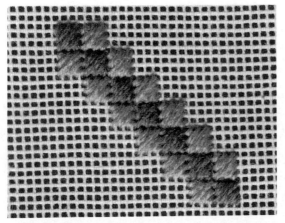

# *Scotch-continuous*

## STITCH NO 24
### STITCH IMPACT – MEDIUM

Flows well, but it does distort the canvas. Work on a working frame. Can be used in rural or city scenes and in children's designs. It does not need a very large area for the stitch to show up at its best.

**Technique:** This is a continuous scotch stitch with no gaps. (1) is over one mesh, (2) is directly below and over two mesh, (3) is directly below (2) and over three mesh. (4) is to the right of (3) and over two mesh, (5) is to the right of (4) and over one mesh. (6) is directly below (5) and over two mesh. It continues in this regular scotch pattern. In the 2nd row the shortest stitch (a) meets (3) the longest stitch of the first row. The row continues as before. You will note that the shortest and longest stitches always meet the longest and shortest stitches of the previous row. Can be worked down and up the canvas.

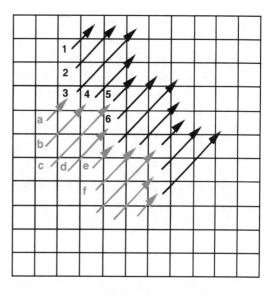

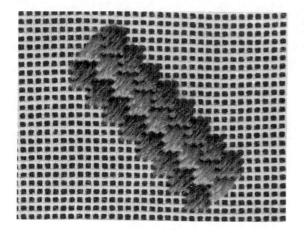

# Scotch-horizontal

STITCH NO 25
STITCH IMPACT – MEDIUM

In some instances it will be more convenient to stitch the scotch units in this way, especially when you want a horizontal border stitch. Distortion of the canvas can occur so, if you are working a large area, use a working frame.

**Technique:** The scotch units are worked next to one another across the canvas. (1, 2, 3, 4, 5) show the position of the first scotch unit. (6, 7) show the commencement of the second scotch unit. The units proceed in this way. In the 2nd row (a) meets (4), (b) meets (5), (c, d, e) complete the unit. (f, g) show the position of the next unit. The units fit next to one another across the canvas. The rows proceed in this way. They are square boxes stitched next to one another.

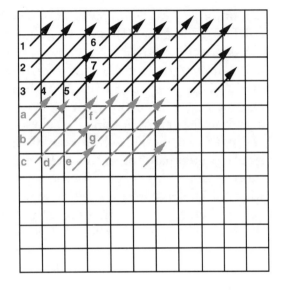

# Scotch-reverse

STITCH NO 26

STITCH IMPACT – MEDIUM

The canvas does not distort as the scotch is pulling in two different directions. There is a hole formed where the 4 units meet. This gives a lighter look to the scotch stitch. The units can be larger. I have seen a French knot placed in this hole – it looks good.

**Technique:** This is the basic scotch unit. (1) is over one mesh, (2) is directly below and over two mesh, (3) is directly below and over three mesh, (4 and 5) move to the right over two mesh and one mesh. There is a skip hole on the diagonal and the unit is repeated. These units continue diagonally down the canvas. In the 2nd row (a, b, c, d, e etc.) is the basic scotch unit worked in the opposite direction. (a) begins six threads from (1). There is a skip hole between each unit. These units continue diagonally down the canvas. The stitching can be done down or up the canvas.

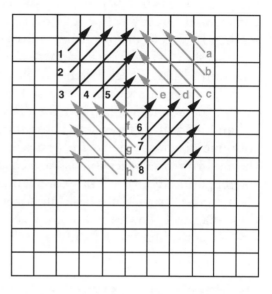

# *Scotch-reverse variation*

## STITCH NO 27
### STITCH IMPACT – MEDIUM

The canvas does not distort as the scotch is pulling in two different directions. The back stitch in the middle of the scotch unit gives the stitch an interesting variation.

**Technique:** This is larger than the basic scotch unit. (1) is over one mesh, (2) commenced directly below it is over two mesh, (3) directly below again and over three mesh, (4, 5, 6, 7) are over one mesh and worked like a back stitch. (8, 9, 10) move to the right over three, two and one mesh. There is a skip hole on the diagonal and the unit is repeated. These units continue diagonally down the canvas. In the 2nd row the same unit is worked in the opposite direction. (a) commences eight threads from (1). These units continue diagonally down the canvas. Can be worked down and up the canvas.

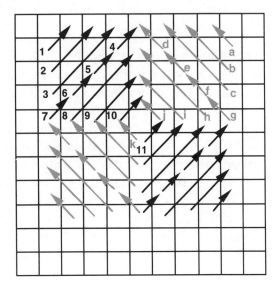

# Scotch-vertical

STITCH NO 28

STITCH IMPACT – MEDIUM

In some instances, it will be more convenient to work the scotch units in this way, especially when you want a vertical border. Distortion can occur, so it is a good idea to use a working frame.

**Technique:** The basic scotch units are worked vertically down the canvas. (1, 2, 3, 4, 5) show the position of the first scotch unit. (6, 7, 8) show the beginning of the second unit below the first. In the 2nd row (a, b, c, d, e) show the position of the second unit with (a) commencing three threads from (1) and meeting (4). (b) meets (5). (c, d, e) complete the second unit. (f, g, h) show the beginning of the next unit. The rows proceed in this way. They are square boxes stitched below one another.

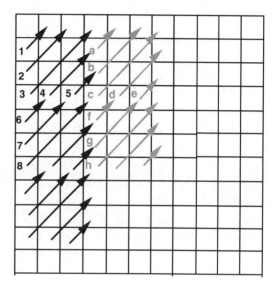

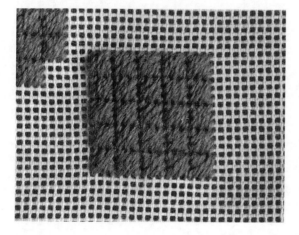

# Scotch checker

STITCH NO 29

STITCH IMPACT – MEDIUM

An interesting variation to both scotch and tent. It gives a two-dimensional effect. Two colours show it up to advantage. Good background in one colour. It does distort so needs to be a worked on a working frame. Suitable for landscapes, town scenes, gardens etc.

**Technique:** The basic scotch unit is separated by nine tent-basketweave stitches (1) is over one mesh (2) is below it and over two mesh (3) is below (2) and over three mesh (4, 5) move to the right of (3) over two mesh and one mesh. (6 to 14) are the tent stitches (15) commences the scotch unit again which alternates with the tent stitches. The 2nd row has the tent stitches under the scotch units and the scotch units under the tent stitches. Can work from either side of the canvas. When working from the right side of the canvas the scotch sequence can be (5, 4, 3, 2, 1) followed by the tent-basketweave stitches.

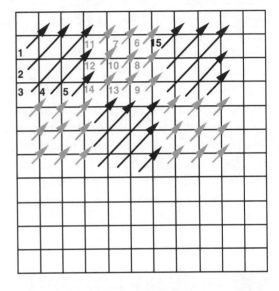

# *Stem*

STITCH NO 30

STITCH IMPACT – LIGHT

Good for columns, fence posts, telegraph poles, masts. Anywhere where a straight effect is called for. Looks good in two colours with a contrasting back stitch.

**Technique:** (1) is over two mesh. (2) is directly below (1) and over two mesh. (3, 4, 5, 6, etc.) follow down the canvas. The 2nd row is the other arm of the first row. (7) meets up with (1) and goes over two mesh in the opposite direction. (8 etc.) follow down the canvas. Very often canvas shows where the two arms meet and, if so, a back stitch (a, b, c etc.) can be put in. Can be worked from either side of the canvas.

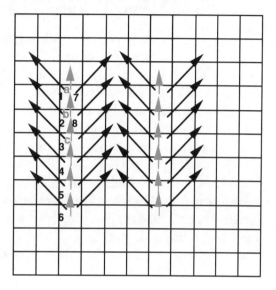

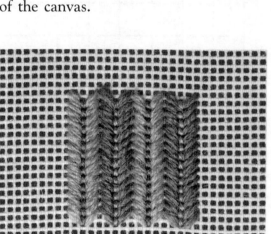

# T stitch

STITCH NO 31

STITCH IMPACT – LIGHT

Used when you want a light, airy stitch where the exposed canvas forms a part of the created pattern. Due to the fact it moves in two directions, very little distortion occurs. An unobtrusive background stitch.

**Technique:** A tent-continental stitch worked in two different directions. (1) covers one mesh of canvas. Miss a mesh and place (2). Miss a mesh and place (3) etc. Shape stitch from bottom left to top right. Continue in this manner. The shape of the stitches in the 2nd row (a, b, c, etc.) is worked in the opposite direction. The shape of the stitch is from bottom right to top left. This row forms a slanted T with the row above. The 3rd row is as the 1st forming a slanted T with the 2nd row. The rows continue in this manner.

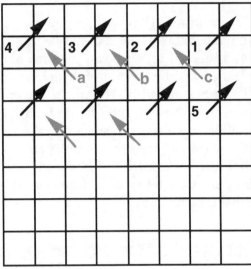

# Tent-basketweave

STITCH NO 32

STITCH IMPACT – LIGHT

Easier to work this stitch in larger areas. For the small areas, tent-continental mixes well with it. No distortion as the vertical and horizontal lines on the back pull against one another. Use this version of basic tent whenever possible.

**Technique:** (1) covers one mesh, (2) is placed to the left of (1) and (3) is directly below (1). (4) is below (3). (5) fills the gap left by (2 and 3). (6) brings you to the top again. (7) is to the left of (6) and (8, 9, 10) fill the gaps on the downward trip. The stitch proceeds diagonally up and down the canvas. If you look at the back of the work you will see that, when working down the canvas, you have a vertical line and working up the canvas, a horizontal line. Check the back regularly to make sure you alternate vertical and horizontal rows. If this is not done, the front will have an uneven look.

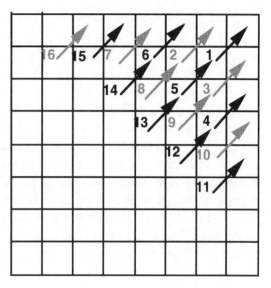

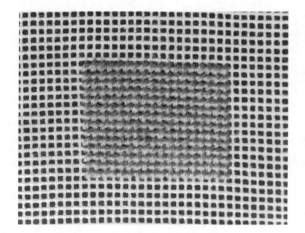

# *Tent-continental*

## STITCH NO 33
### STITCH IMPACT – LIGHT

This makes an excellent background stitch **but** it distorts the canvas. The distortion is less if the stitching is done on a working frame. The stitch at the back of the canvas is strong and durable.

**Technique:** A(1) worked from right to left of canvas – shape of the stitch, bottom left to top right. Return row canvas can be turned upside down as in A(1) (a, b) or change the direction of the stitch from top right to bottom left as in A(2) (a, b), **always** still the same diagonal shape. B(1) worked from top to bottom, return row canvas can be turned upside down as in B(1) (a, b) or change the direction of stitch from top right to bottom left, as in B(2) (a, b). C is worked diagonally from the left side of the canvas, D is worked diagonally from the right side of the canvas.

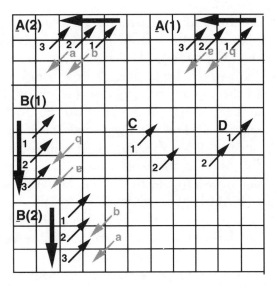

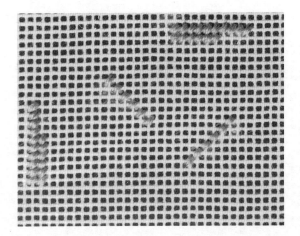

# *Tent-continental irregular*

## STITCH NO 34
### STITCH IMPACT – MEDIUM

The stitch at the back of the canvas is very thick. The random look of this stitch allows it to be used in areas that are not too regimented. I have seen it used on a goose's back most successfully!

**Technique:** This stitch is worked in the same way as tent-continental. The difference is that the stitch can be of any length. The length is counted by the number of mesh crossed by each tent-continental. In the 2nd row (a, b, c etc.) the method of stitching is reversed to give the correct backing. It is not advisable to make the stitches too long as they can snag. I have shown random lengths for each row. You can either follow my diagram or proceed to make the stitches the length you wish.

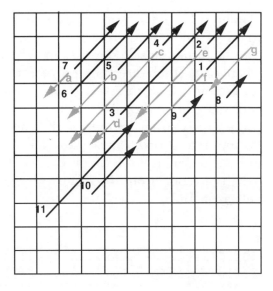

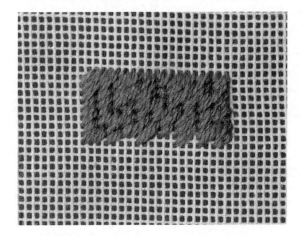

# Tent-half cross

STITCH NO 35

STITCH IMPACT – LIGHT

This way of working tent stitch should be avoided unless working on a 'trammed' canvas, or on a picture using penelope canvas. There is no thickness of wool on the back thus providing insufficient durability or strength for cushions or chair covers.

**Technique:** A(1) worked from left to right of the canvas; return row, canvas can be turned upside down as in A(1) or change the stitch direction from top right to bottom left as in A(2). (N.B. Always still the same diagonal shape.)

B(1) worked from bottom of the canvas to top; return row, canvas can be turned upside down as in B(1) or change the stitch direction from top right to bottom left as in B(2).

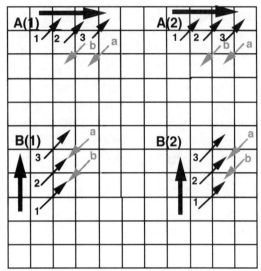

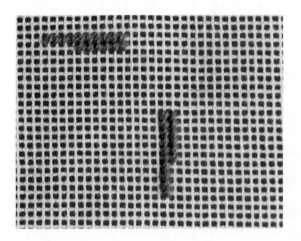

# Tent-reverse

## STITCH NO 36
## STITCH IMPACT – LIGHT

A good background stitch, light and airy, as the canvas is sparsely covered. It does not distort as the movement of the stitches are in two different directions.

**Technique:** This stitch is worked diagonally down and up the canvas allowing for a missed mesh between each part. (1) covers one mesh (2) is placed two mesh of canvas away from (1) and proceeds diagonally down the canvas. (5) is placed two mesh of canvas away from (4) and proceeds diagonally up the canvas. The rows proceed down and up in this way. In the 2nd row (a) commences at (1) but is stitched in the opposite direction from bottom right to top left. (b) meets (a). It is worked as a back stitch. (c) starts at (2). (d, e, f) follow. Rows alternate in this way.

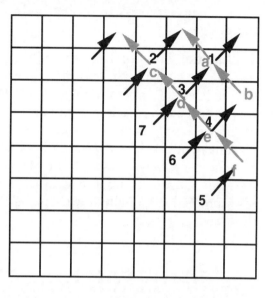

# *Tent-skip*

## STITCH NO 37
## STITCH IMPACT – LIGHT

The canvas is a part of the effect created by this stitch. It is better done on a fine canvas as too much heavy canvas showing would not look good. Used correctly it gives a light, airy look to bushes and trees and is a background stitch that enhances the design.

**Technique:** This stitch is worked diagonally down and up the canvas, allowing for a missed mesh between each part. (1) covers one mesh, (2) is placed two mesh of canvas away from (1) and proceeds diagonally down the canvas. (5) is placed two mesh of canvas away from (4) and proceeds diagonally up the canvas. The rows proceed diagonally down and up in this way.

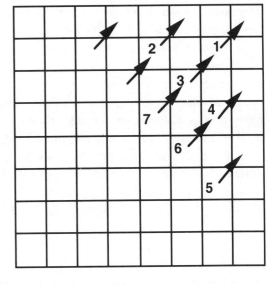

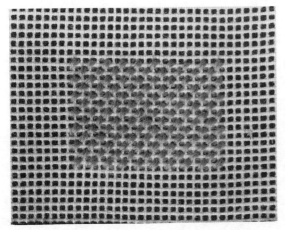

# STRAIGHT FAMILY

## *Algerian*

### STITCH NO 38
### STITCH IMPACT – LIGHT

Can span a desired, even number of threads, so can go from light to heavy impact depending on the size of the stitches used. Each unit can be as many stitches as required. Useful for roof shingles and for stone work.

**Technique:** (1) the stitch is over two threads of canvas. (2 and 3) parallel to (1). (4) goes across and down one thread of canvas from (3). (5 and 6) are parallel to (4). (7) moves up and across one thread of canvas from (6). The stitch units have three stitches to each unit. In the 2nd row (a) comes up two threads from (1) and goes up to meet (1). (b and c) are parallel to (a). This, and subsequent rows, follow the pattern set by the 1st row. The stitch can be worked from either side of the canvas.

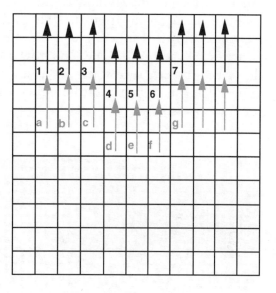

# Algerian-horizontal

STITCH NO 39

STITCH IMPACT – LIGHT

The number of threads spanned by each stitch can increase as long as they remain even. Each unit can be as many stitches as required. Effective for the sides and roofs of houses.

**Technique:** The stitch units are the same as Algerian, running horizontally instead of vertically. (1) the stitch is over two threads of canvas. (2, 3) are parallel to (1). (4) moves down and across one thread of canvas from (3). (5, 6) are parallel to (4). (7) moves down and across one thread of canvas from (6). The units continue in this manner. There are three stitches to each unit. The 2nd row follows the pattern set by the 1st row etc. The stitch can be worked from either end of the canvas.

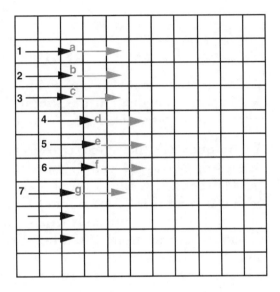

# *Brick*

STITCH NO 40

STITCH IMPACT – LIGHT

Brick is a versatile stitch as it can be worked over two or more threads of canvas. The bigger the size of the stitch, the more impact is created. Therefore, it can go from a light to a heavy impact, depending on the size.

**Technique:** (1) The stitch is over two threads of the canvas. (2) moves up across and up one thread of canvas. It is over two threads of canvas. The stitch continues across the canvas moving up and down in this way. In the 2nd row (a) commences two threads down from (1) and meets (1). (b, c, d etc.) move up and down the canvas, meeting the first row and following the pattern set by it. The rows continue in this way. The stitch can be worked from either side of the canvas.

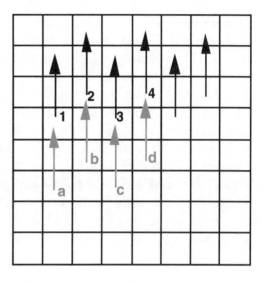

# Brick-giant

STITCH NO 41

STITCH IMPACT – HEAVY

The heavy impact of the stitch makes it unsuitable for small background areas. This stitch is fast to work, but it is large and can be snagged. It gives an elongated look to your work.

**Technique:** This is a larger version of brick stitch. (1) is up over four threads of canvas. (2) is across one thread and up two threads of canvas. It is over four threads. (3) is down two threads of canvas and across one thread and goes up over four threads. The stitches continue up and down the canvas in this way. The 2nd row (a) comes up four threads down from (1). (b, c, d, etc.) move up and down the canvas meeting the first row. The rows continue in this way. The stitch can be worked from either side of the canvas.

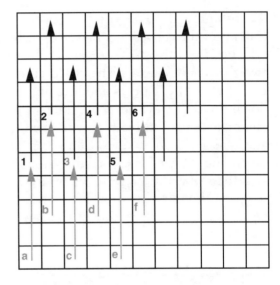

# *Brick-horizontal*

STITCH NO 42

STITCH IMPACT – LIGHT

This is a good background stitch. Gives a distinct horizontal look, so works well for the sides of buildings, also for paths or roads.

**Technique:** Brick-horizontal is worked down the canvas. (1) The stitch is over two threads of the canvas. (2) moves down and across one thread of canvas. It is over two threads of canvas. The stitch zig-zags down the canvas in this fashion. The 2nd row (a) commences two threads across from (1). (b, c, d etc.) follow the pattern set by the 1st row. The rows continue across the canvas in this way. Can be worked either down or up the canvas.

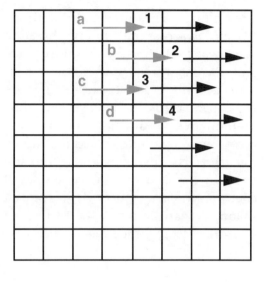

# *Flame*

STITCH NO 43
STITCH IMPACT – MEDIUM

A stitch in the bargello family. The lst row creates the pattern which is followed by each row. Looks good in toning colours. A good background stitch in one colour.

**Technique:** (1) is up over four threads. (2) moves across and up one thread and goes over four threads. (3) moves across and up one thread and goes over four threads. This is as tall as the stitch gets. (4) moves across and down one thread and up over four threads. (5) moves across and down one thread and up over four threads. This is as low as the stitch goes. In the 2nd row (a) comes up and over four threads to meet (1). (c, d, e etc.) follow the pattern set by the 1st row. Can be worked from either side of the canvas.

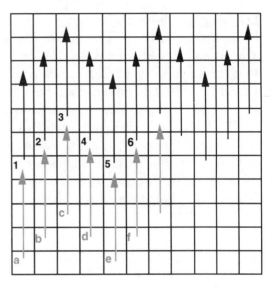

# *Flame-variation*

STITCH NO 44

STITCH IMPACT – MEDIUM

Makes a lovely background stitch. The effect is altered when a second colour is used for the dividing stitch between the rows of flame.

**Technique:** (1) is up over four threads. (2) moves across and up one thread of canvas and goes over four threads. (3) moves across and up one thread and goes over four threads. (4) starts the downward journey. The flame part of the stitch is formed. (a, b, c, d etc.) are over two threads of canvas and follow the pattern set by the flame. This forms a break row between the rows of flame. In the 3rd row, the flame is repeated, following the set pattern. The rows alternate. Can be worked from either side of the canvas.

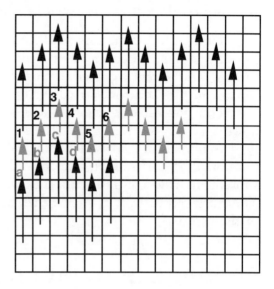

# *Gobelin-split*

## STITCH NO 45
### STITCH IMPACT – LIGHT

A tight stitch which can be worked over two or more even threads of canvas. However, it is not a good idea to have the stitch too large. Do not have the fibre you use too thin, because it will be difficult to split.

**Technique:** (1, 2, 3 etc) are worked next to one another and cover two threads of canvas. The stitches proceed across the canvas. In the 2nd row (a) comes up in the empty hole directly below (1) and goes down into the middle of (1), still covering two threads of canvas. This row splits the fibre of the 1st row (a, b, c etc). Each subsequent row continues in this way. The stitch can be worked from either side of the canvas.

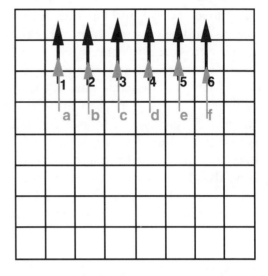

# *Gobelin-straight*

STITCH NO 46

STITCH IMPACT – LIGHT

Can be stitched over any number of threads. If the stitches are pulled too tight, a gap is formed between the rows. A back stitch can be worked between the rows if necessary. Useful for interpreting straight lines.

**Technique:** (1, 2, 3 etc) are worked next to one another and cover two threads of canvas. In the 2nd row (a) commences two threads of canvas below (1) and meets it. (b, c, d etc.) follow on. The 2nd row shares the holes with the 1st row. Each subsequent row meets the row above.

The stitch can be worked from either side of the canvas. It can also be turned sideways and worked down and up the canvas.

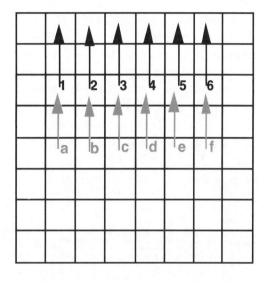

# *Gobelin-straight interlock*

## STITCH NO 47
## STITCH IMPACT – LIGHT

The fibre for this stitch should not be too thick. This is a tight stitch, useful for small areas. Better for using in design areas rather than in background areas.

**Technique:** The four stitches (1, 2, 3, 4) are over two threads of canvas and next to one another. In the 2nd row (a) comes up directly below (1) and goes up over two threads of canvas. It fits between (1 and 2). (b, c, d etc.) continue in this manner. The 3rd row meets the 1st row and the 4th row meets the 2nd row. The stitch continues like this. It can be worked from either side of the canvas.

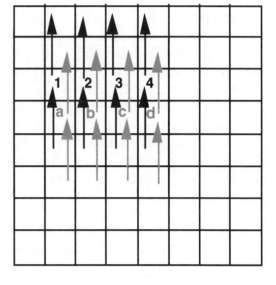

# *Hungarian*

STITCH NO 48

STITCH IMPACT – LIGHT

A small, vertical, diamond effect is created by this stitch. It is a great background stitch that looks wonderful in one colour. Takes on a completely different look in two colours. Can also be used in small design areas.

**Technique:** (1) goes up over two threads. (2) drops down and across one thread and goes up over four threads. (3) moves across and up one thread and goes up over two threads. A hole is skipped and the unit of three parts is repeated etc. In the 2nd row, (a) comes up two threads down from (3) and meets (3). (b) drops down and across one thread and goes over four threads. It fills the skip hole. (c) meets (4). There is a skip hole before the next unit is placed. Can be worked from either side of the canvas.

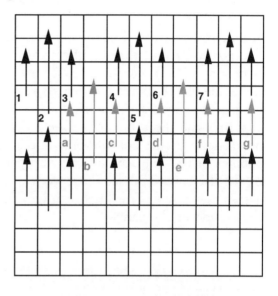

# Hungarian-double

### STITCH NO 49
### STITCH IMPACT – MEDIUM

An elongated horizontal look is achieved with this stitch. Can be stitched in different colours for an unusual striped effect. Nice for a sky – try blending colours.

**Technique:** (1, 2) are side by side over two threads of canvas. (3) drops down and across one thread of canvas from (2) and goes over four threads of canvas. (4) is next to (3). (5, 6) are as (1, 2) on the right side of (4). There are two skip holes before the sequence is repeated. In the 2nd row, the short stitches of the 1st row have short stitches below them. The long stitches of the 2nd row fill the skip gaps of the 1st row. The sequence continues across the canvas. The stitch can be from either side of the canvas.

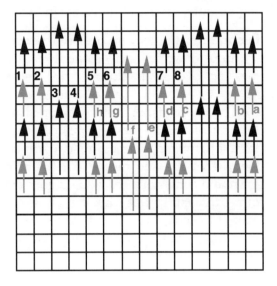

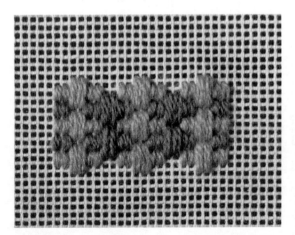

# Hungarian-ground

STITCH NO 50

STITCH IMPACT – MEDIUM

A smooth and elegant stitch – good for backgrounds and design areas. The stitch changes character if the Hungarian unit is in a different colour or fibre.

**Technique:** A combination of two units. (1, 2, 3, 4 etc.) is a flame pattern moving up and down the canvas in one-step movements. (2) is one thread across and up from (1), (3) is one thread across and up from (2). (4) is one thread of canvas down from (3) etc. In the 2nd row (a) is over two threads of canvas (b) over 4 threads and (c) over two threads. This Hungarian unit fills the centre of the flames. The 3rd row is as the lst, moving down and up the canvas meeting the 1st row every fourth stitch. The odd rows enclose the Hungarian unit. Can be worked from either side of the canvas.

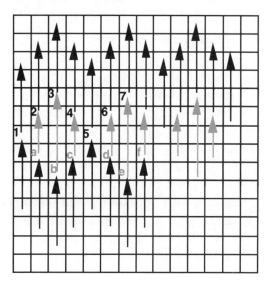

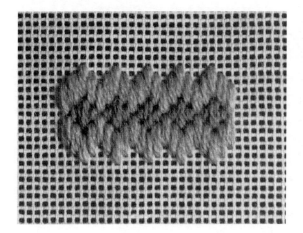

# Hungarian-horizontal

STITCH NO 51

STITCH IMPACT – LIGHT

A small diamond effect but this time on the horizontal instead of the vertical. Works well as a background. Good for the sky and the sea, especially with the colours blended.

**Technique:** (1) goes across two threads. (2) moves down and across to the left one thread and goes over four threads. (3) moves down and across to the right one thread and goes over two threads. A hole is skipped and the unit of three parts is repeated etc. (a) comes up two threads from (3) and meets (3). (b) drops down and across one thread and goes over four threads. It fills the skip hole. (c) meets (4) and there is a skip hole before the next unit is placed. Can be worked from either side of the canvas.

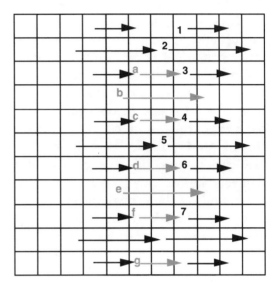

# Milanese-vertical

STITCH NO 52

STITCH IMPACT – MEDIUM

An attractive stitch which covers the canvas quickly. Gives an effective vertical look and is a smart background stitch. Looks good with the filling stitch in a different colour and/or a different fibre.

**Technique:** (1) is over six threads of canvas (2) is across and up one thread from (1) and over four threads, (3) is across and up one thread from (2) and over two threads. This completes the sequence. (4) is across three threads from (1) and the sequence is repeated. It continues in this way. The 3rd row is the same as the 1st with the six thread stitches meeting one another. (a, b) fill the gaps created by the 1st and 3rd rows. The Milanese sequence creates the gaps to be filled with the (a, b) stitches.

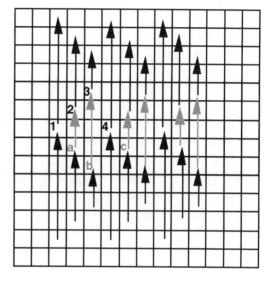

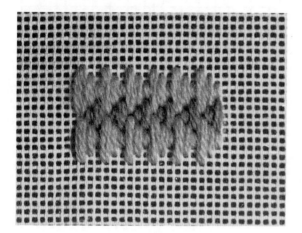

# *Old Florentine*

## STITCH NO 53
### STITCH IMPACT – MEDIUM

A stitch from the bargello family. Looks good when used for a large wall or the side of a large building. The fact that it covers six threads of canvas makes it larger than most of the other straight stitches. Can be worked on the horizontal as well as the vertical.

**Technique:** (1) is over six threads. (2) is next to and parallel to (1). (3) is across one and up two threads from (2). (4) is next to (3). The stitch continues across the canvas in this way. In the 2nd row (a) comes up two threads down from (1) and meets (1). (b) is parallel to (a). (c) comes up six threads down from (3) and meets (3). (d) is next to (c). The long and short of the 1st row meet the short and long of the 2nd row. The stitches and rows proceed in this way. Can be worked from either side of the canvas.

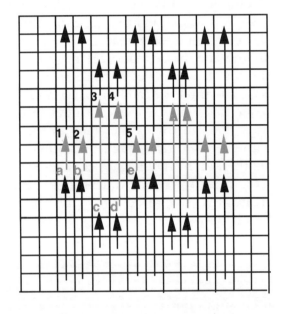

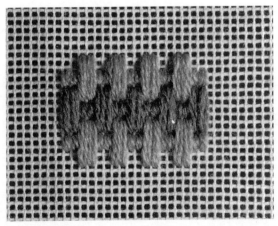

# Parisian

STITCH NO 54

STITCH IMPACT – LIGHT

A good background stitch, not too dominant, and is quite quick to stitch. Useful for buildings and anywhere requiring a horizontal line-type look. Appropriate for city and country scenes.

**Technique:** (1) is up over two threads of the canvas, (2) is down and across one thread of canvas and goes up over four threads of canvas. This sequence is repeated across the canvas. In the 2nd row, (a) comes up four threads down from (1) and meets (1), (b) is across and up one thread from (a) and goes over two threads to meet (2) etc. The long and the short of each row meet the opposite length of the next row etc. Can be worked from either side of the canvas.

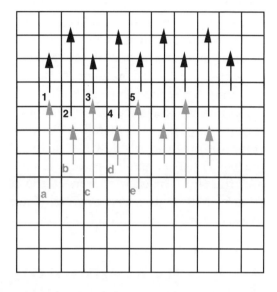

# *Parisian-double*

STITCH NO 55

STITCH IMPACT – MEDIUM

Can be a quickly worked background stitch. Gives a feeling of horizontal length. I have used it on the fuselage of a plane as it has a rather static look.

**Technique:** (1) is up over two threads of canvas (2) is parallel to (1). (3) goes down and across one thread of canvas and is up over four threads of canvas. (4) is parallel to (3). (5) commences the short and long sequence again. In the 2nd row (a) comes up four threads down from (1) and meets (1). (b) is parallel to (a). (c) comes up two threads down from (3) and meets (3). (d) is parallel to (c). The long and the short of each row meet the opposite length of the next row etc. Can be worked from either side of the canvas.

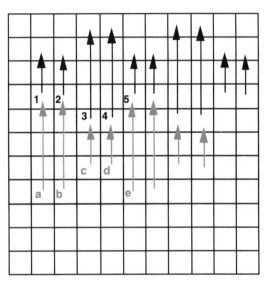

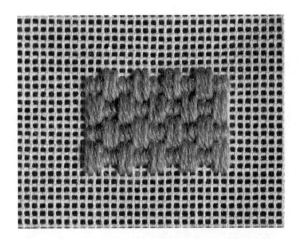

# *Parisian stripe*

STITCH NO 56

STITCH IMPACT – LIGHT

Can form interesting combinations with the use of different fibres in the two parts of the stitch. Wool in the Parisian part and pearl cotton in the stripe are effective. Different colours look good. Can be a good background stitch in one colour.

**Technique:** (1) is up over four threads. (2) moves across and up one thread of canvas and goes up over two threads of canvas. (3) drops down and across one thread of canvas. This is the Parisian part of the stitch. This sequence is repeated across the canvas. In the 2nd row (a) is up over two threads and meets (2). (b) is across two threads of canvas from (a) and goes up over two threads of canvas to meet (4). This row forms the stripe. The 1st and 2nd rows are repeated. Can be worked from either side of the canvas.

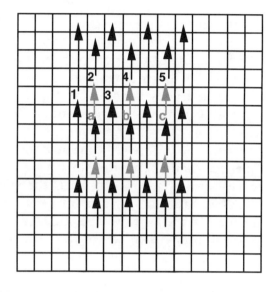

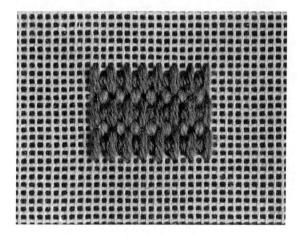

# *Pavilion*

STITCH NO 57

STITCH IMPACT – MEDIUM

Lovely diamond effect. Nice to stitch and gives a pleasant effect. It looks good in two colours. A good background stitch when done in one colour and can be stitched quite quickly. Good for country scenes.

**Technique:** (1) goes up over two threads of canvas. (2) drops down and across one thread and goes up over four threads of canvas. (3) drops down and across one thread and goes up over six threads of canvas. (4) moves across and up one thread of canvas and goes over four threads. (5, 6, 7 etc.) continue the sequence. In the 2nd row (a) meets the largest of the 1st row, (b) meets the middle size of the 1st row and (c) meets the smallest of the 1st row. The stitch can be worked from either side of the canvas.

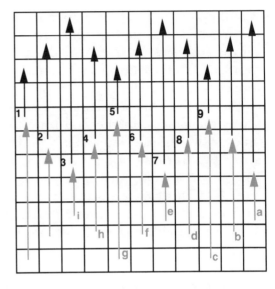

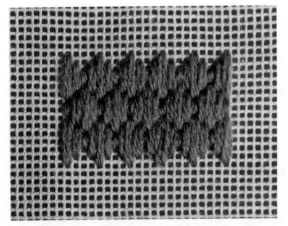

# Pavilion Diamonds

STITCH NO 58

STITCH IMPACT – MEDIUM

Looks good in one colour, making an effective background. A different look is achieved when two colours are used. Because it forms interlocking diamonds, makes wonderful tiles on a roof.

**Technique:** (1) is over two threads of canvas. (2) drops down and across one thread and goes up over four threads of canvas. (3) drops down and across one thread and goes up over six threads of canvas. (4) moves across and up one thread and goes over four threads. (5) is as (1). There is a skip hole and the whole unit is repeated. In the 2nd row the same sequence is followed with the six-thread part of the stitch (e), filling the skip hole of the previous row. Can be worked from either side of the canvas.

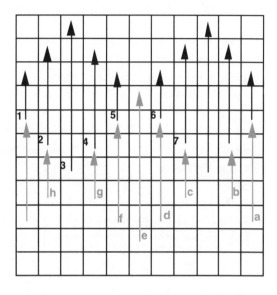

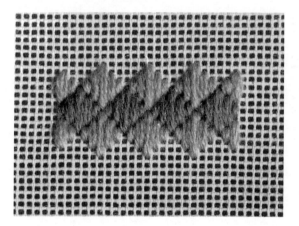

# *Twill*

## STITCH NO 59
### STITCH IMPACT – MEDIUM

This stitch forms diagonal lines across the canvas; on a small canvas it is an effective background. Imagine how good it looks as a diagonal path or road.

**Technique:** (1) is over three threads, (2) drops down and across one thread from (1) and goes up over three threads (3, 4, 5 etc) continue in this manner. In the 2nd row (a) comes up three threads down from (1) and meets (1). (b, c, d, e etc.) drop down in the same manner as the 1st row meeting (2, 3, 4, 5). All ensuing rows follow this set pattern. Can be worked from either side of the canvas.

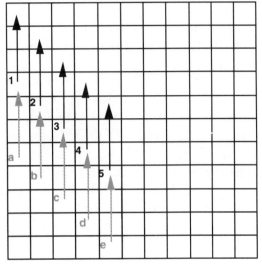

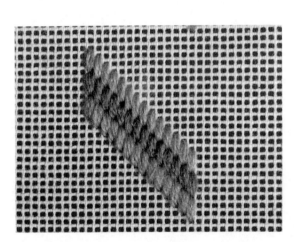

# Victorian step

STITCH NO 60

STITCH IMPACT – MEDIUM

A stepping, straight stitch that gives an angled look. Good for land and seascapes. Suitable for backgrounds.

**Technique:** (1) is up over four threads of canvas. (2) commences directly next to (1) and is over two threads of canvas. (3, 4) are parallel to (2). (5) is down two threads and across one thread from (4). It begins the next group of four stitches. The units continue down the canvas. In the 2nd row (a) is over two threads of canvas and meets (1). (b, c,) are parallel to (a). (d) is down two threads and across one thread from (c). It begins the next group of four stitches. The rows continue in this way.

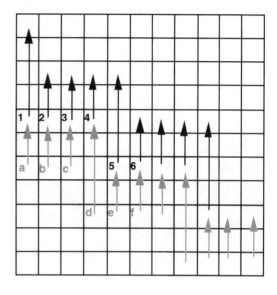

# CROSSED AND COMBINATION FAMILY

## *Cross-3 stitch*

### STITCH NO 61
### STITCH IMPACT – LIGHT

Can be effective worked in two colours with the second colour as the cross bar. It may be necessary to thicken the fibre if the canvas shows through.

**Technique:** Each cross is worked completely as in (1, 2) before moving on to the next one. In the diagram, the left arm of the cross has been worked first each time. It is essential to keep the same arms, in this case (2, 4, 6) on the top all the time. The straight stitch on the top (a, b, c, d) is worked as a back stitch.

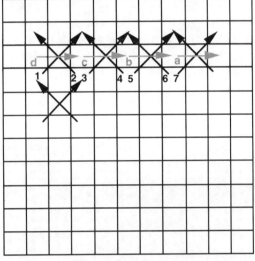

# Cross-broad

STITCH NO 62

STITCH IMPACT – HEAVY

A cross stitch that stands very well on its own and could be used in geometric designs. In different colours, could be stylised flowers. Would be good as a border stitch.

**Technique:** (1) is over three mesh. (2) is to the left of (1) and over four mesh. (3) is above (2) and over three mesh. Drop down four threads from the top of (3) to commence (4) which is over three mesh. (5) is to the right of (4) and over four mesh. (6) is above (5) and over three mesh. A broad cross is formed. The units are placed next to one another. For uniformity make sure (4, 5, 6) are always on top of (1, 2, 3).

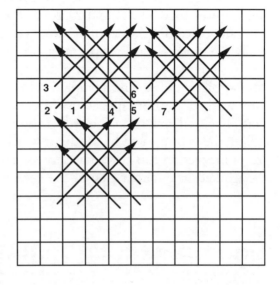

# *Cross-double*

## STITCH NO 63
## STITCH IMPACT – MEDIUM

Has a star-like quality and I use it mainly in this context. Can also be used for flowers. Looks good with the rows alternating in colour.

**Technique:** Formed by using two different crosses together. (1 and 2) cover four threads of canvas horizontally and vertically. (3 and 4) cover two mesh diagonally and are placed over the centre of the straight cross. The complete crosses are worked horizontally across the canvas. The 2nd row is positioned as shown, filling the gaps created by the 1st row. The rows proceed in this way. The crosses can be worked from either side of the canvas.

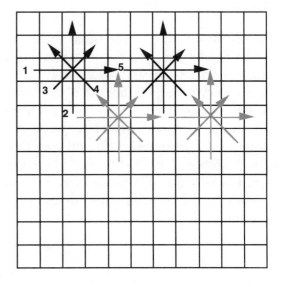

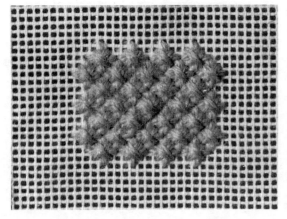

# Cross-oblong

STITCH NO 64

STITCH IMPACT – LIGHT

A small stitch which can be used in small, detailed areas. Gives a slightly elongated effect. Could be suitable for a garden, for boats or interior scenes.

**Technique:** This cross is not at a 45° angle. It is a slanted cross. It is up over two threads of canvas and across one thread. Each cross is worked completely (1, 2) before moving on to the next one. In the diagram, the left arm of the cross has been worked first each time. It is essential to keep the same arm, in this case (2, 4, 6), on the top all the time. Oblong crosses can be worked from either side of the canvas.

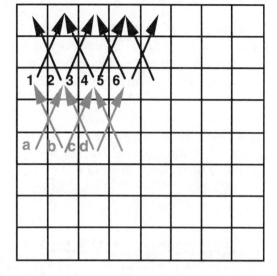

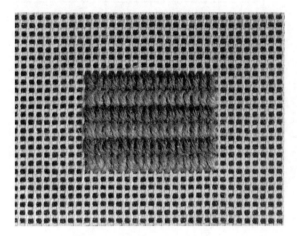

# Cross-straight

STITCH NO 65

STITCH IMPACT – LIGHT

A tight, small stitch which gives a nubbly effect. Excellent where you want the look of stonework. Could use a blended fibre or a different colour for the top part of the cross.

**Technique:** A straight cross worked in horizontal rows. (1, 2) go over two threads vertically and horizontally. They are positioned next to one another and the horizontal part of the stitch shares the horizontal part of the stitch before it. The 2nd row fills the gaps created by the 1st row. The rows proceed in this way. The crosses can be worked from either side of the canvas.

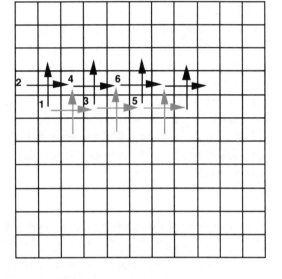

# Cross-straight long

## STITCH NO 66
## STITCH IMPACT – LIGHT

The stitch gives an interesting tied look and can work in small areas. You will need to make sure the canvas is covered by the stitch. This may require increasing the strands of fibre used.

**Technique:** (1) goes up over four threads of canvas. (2) comes up one thread across and two threads up from (1). (3) commences two threads down and one thread across from (1) meeting (2). (4) is placed the same way as (2). The stitches move up and down in this manner. In the 2nd row (a) is four threads down from the first part of the cross and comes up to meet it. (b) covers (a) as in the previous row. (c) is placed as was (3). The stitches move up and down in this manner, linking up with the previous row.

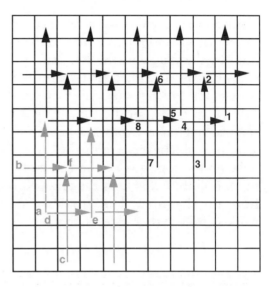

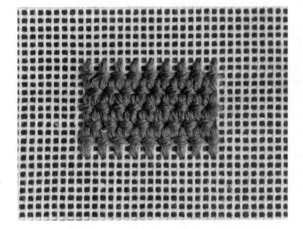

# Cross stitch

### STITCH NO 67
### STITCH IMPACT – LIGHT

Many other crossed stitches have this cross as the base. It is a neat stitch and good for small areas. For canvas work I find it better to work a complete cross before moving on to the next one. The crosses can be made larger, if required.

**Technique:** Each cross is worked completely (1, 2) before moving on to the next one. In the diagram, the left arm of the cross has been worked first each time. It is essential to keep the same arm, in this case (2, 4, 6, 8), on the top all the time. It does not have to always be the right arm, but whichever arm of the cross you have on the top, this arm must be on the top for all the other crosses. The 2nd row fits into the first. The crosses can be worked from either side of the canvas.

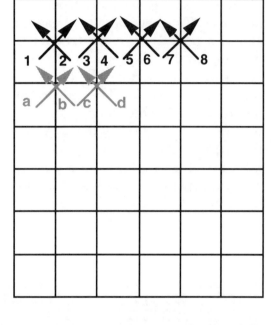

# Crossed gobelin

## STITCH NO 68
## STITCH IMPACT – MEDIUM

This stitch is quick and easy to work and makes a firm, three-dimensional stitch. Can create a textured feature in a scene. Will act as a large filling stitch in a large area. Walls of stone buildings spring to mind.

**Technique:** (1) is over six threads of canvas, (2, 3) cross the two mesh in the middle of the straight stitch. (4) commences two threads across from (1) and (5, 6) cross (4) as before. The units progress across the canvas in this way. (a) commences four threads down one thread across from (1). It finishes in the same hole as (2 and 6). (b, c) cross (a) as before. This 2nd row fills the gaps created by the 1st row. The rows follow in this way. Can be worked from either side of the canvas.

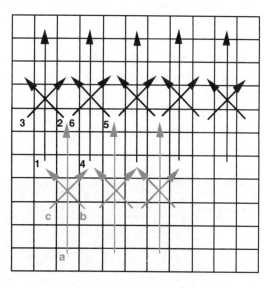

# Crossmix

## STITCH NO 69
### STITCH IMPACT – LIGHT

Two colours look good in this stitch. You will need to experiment with the number of strands of wool or cotton you use.

**Technique:** The crosses are worked doing the left arm first (1, 2, 3, 4) – they are over two mesh. The right arm (5, 6 etc) is placed on the top of the left arm on the return journey. Each row of crosses meets the previous row. The straight crosses (a, b, c, d etc.) are placed after the completion of the crossed crosses.

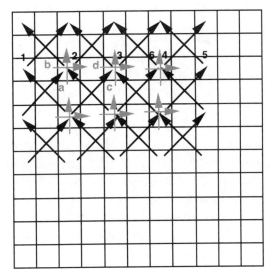

# Diamond ray

STITCH NO 70

STITCH IMPACT – MEDIUM

Has an interesting look and is great when leaves or flowers are required. They can vary in colour for a garden effect.

**Technique:** Each part of the stitch goes into the same hole. (1) is over four threads of canvas. (2) is two mesh down from (1) on the left and goes over two mesh. (3) is two mesh down from (1) on the right side and goes over two mesh. (4, 5) are one mesh down from (1) on each side of it and go down into the same hole. (6) commences four threads across from (1) and the whole sequence is repeated. The 2nd row fits the same unit between those of the 1st. row. The rows proceed in this way.

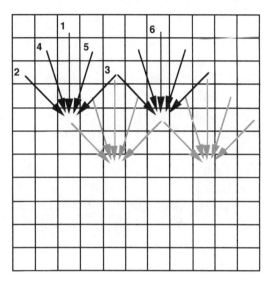

# Leviathan double

STITCH NO 71

STITCH IMPACT – HEAVY

A heavy stitch that looks good when used in conjunction with flatter stitches. Effective as part of a garden scene. Looks good in geometric designs. Works well as a border stitch.

**Technique:** (1 to 2) is over four mesh. (3 to 4) is commenced four threads across from (1) and completes the cross. Follow the numbers in sequence to create this stitch. Every hole around the square is filled. The second stitch is placed directly next to the first and shares holes with it. The 2nd row stitches are directly below the 1st row and they share holes. Make sure the arms of the crosses are placed in sequence. Can be worked from either side of the canvas.

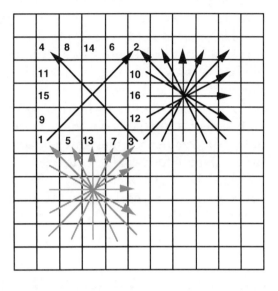

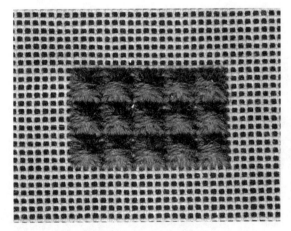

# Long-armed cross stitch

STITCH NO 72

STITCH IMPACT – LIGHT

The main use of this stitch for me is as a binding stitch to bind the edge of a stitched piece or to bind two stitched edges together. I have explained this usage at the end of the Rainbow Houses. The stitch can be used to create straight lines.

**Technique:** The stitch commences with a cross over two mesh (1, 2). (3) commences back at (1) and goes up two threads and across four threads. It is the long-arm part of the stitch. (4) commences two threads down from the end of (3) and is a normal cross arm going over two mesh. Drop down two threads to (5) and place the long-arm. The stitch proceeds in this fashion. To turn the corner, turn the canvas and place the cross (a, b) after the last long-arm. This starts you off in the next direction.

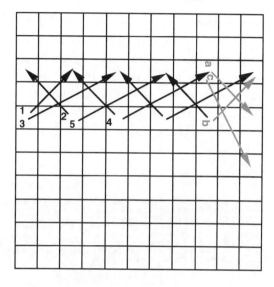

# Mary Rhodes stitch

STITCH NO 73

STITCH IMPACT – HEAVY

Called after the creator of the stitch, Mary Rhodes. An attractive centre for many geometric designs. Can also work nicely in a border. It does have a definite dimensional effect.

**Technique:** The first part of the stitch is from (1 to 2). The stitch then proceeds anti-clockwise around the square, following the number sequence. In this instance, the stitch is worked over an eight-thread square, but it can be over any number of threads. It becomes unwieldy if it is too large.

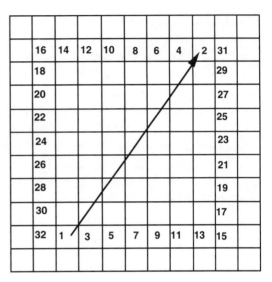

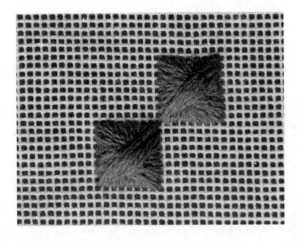

# *Rice*

### STITCH NO 74
### STITCH IMPACT – LIGHT

Looks good in one colour and completely different if a second colour is used for the corner cross bars. Not good for backgrounds as there are too many movements to the stitch. A good geometric and border stitch.

**Technique:** Each cross over two mesh is worked completely (1, 2, a, b, c, d) before moving on to the next one. Make sure there is no gap of canvas between the stitches. The stitch can be worked from either side of the canvas. The 2nd row here has been shown coming from the opposite side of the canvas.

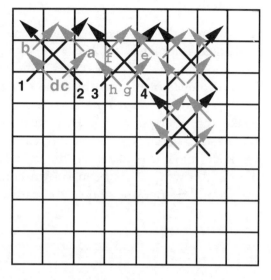

# Rice-giant

## STITCH NO 75
### STITCH IMPACT – MEDIUM

Most effective when done with two colours. Not as useful as rice because of its size. However, the attributes of the stitch show better in this size. A good geometric and border stitch. The stitch does not have much fibre on the back, so does not have good durability.

**Technique:** Each cross over four mesh is worked completely (1, 2, a, b, c, d) before moving on to the next one. The (a, b, c, d) order on this giant version of rice is slightly different from the small rice. Make sure there is no gap of canvas between the stitches. The stitch can be worked from either side of the canvas. The 2nd row here has been shown coming from the opposite side of the canvas.

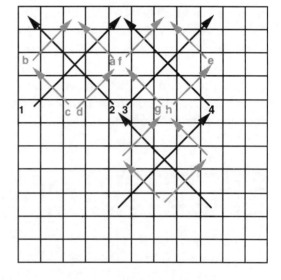

# Smyrna cross

STITCH NO 76

STITCH IMPACT – LIGHT

I have said it has a light impact as it is a small stitch. However, it does stand away from the canvas so gives a three-dimensional effect. A small border stitch that looks good with flat stitches next to it.

**Technique:** Each part of the stitch is completed before moving on to the next one. (1, 2) is the crossed part of the stitch and (a, b) is the straight cross that is worked on the top of the crossed cross. The crosses fit next to one another. Make sure there is no gap of canvas between the Smyrna crosses. The stitch can be worked from either side of the canvas.

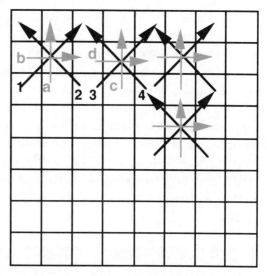

# Waffle

## STITCH NO 77
### STITCH IMPACT – HEAVY

A textured stitch which looks good in the centre of a geometric design. I have used it over seven mesh, but it could be larger as long as it is over an odd number. To my mind, it will snag if it is too big.

**Technique:** (1, 2) is over seven mesh. (3, 4) commences seven threads across from (1) and goes over seven mesh. Follow the anti-clockwise numbers in sequence to create this stitch. The stitch gives a woven appearance as it is worked. The waffles are worked either next to one another or above or below one another. When there is more than one waffle, they will share holes so that no canvas is left between them.

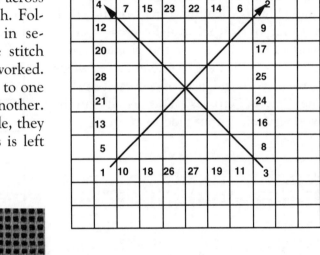

# CHAPTER 8

# DESIGNS

## Rainbow Sampler

| | | | | |
|---|---|---|---|---|
| **1**<br>(3) | **2**<br>(2) | **3**<br>(2) | **4**<br>(2) | **5**<br>(3) |
| **6**<br>yellow (2)<br>green (1) | **7**<br>(2) | **8**<br>(3) | **9**<br>(2) | **10**<br>(2) |
| **11**<br>(3) | **12**<br>(2) | **C**<br>(2) | **13**<br>(3) | **14**<br>(2) |
| **15**<br>(2) | **16**<br>(2) | **17**<br>(3) | **18**<br>(1) | **19**<br>(2) |
| **20**<br>(1) | **21**<br>(3) | **22**<br>(2) | **23**<br>(2) | **24**<br>(3) |

(The bracketed figures in the diagram above show number of strands of Persian wool required for each stitch.)

MATERIALS

- 40 cm (16") square #12 mono interlock canvas
- No 20 needle
- Fibre: DMC Floralia Persian Wool: Dark Blue and Yellow, seven skeins each. Mid Blue, Yellow, Orange, Red, Green, four skeins each.

METHOD

    C = tent-basketweave (Stitch No 32) with cross-double (Stitch No 63)

    1 = Brick-giant (Stitch No 41)

    2 = Moorish (Stitch No 15)

    3 = Smyrna (Stitch No 76)

    4 = Mosaic (Stitch No 16)

    5 = Hungarian-ground (Stitch No 50)

    6 = Cross-3 stitch (Stitch No 61)

    7 = Byzantine (Stitch No 1)

    8 = Flame (Stitch No 43)

    9 = Scotch (Stitch No 23)

  10 = Kalem (Stitch No 12)

  11 = Parisian (Stitch No 54)

  12 = Crossmix (Stitch No 69)

  13 = Parisian-double (Stitch No 55)

  14 = Long-armed cross (Stitch No 72)

  15 = Rice-giant (Stitch No 75)

  16 = Nubuko (Stitch No 22)

  17 = Pavilion (Stitch No 57)

  18 = Gobelin-slanted (inter.2x1) (Stitch No 9)

  19 = Jacquard (Stitch No 11)

  20 = Knotted (Stitch No 13)

  21 = Hungarian (Stitch No 48)

  22 = Cross Stitch (Stitch No 67)

  23 = Cashmere (Stitch No 2)

  24 = Brick-horizontal (Stitch No 42)

The sampler is surrounded by eight rows of tent-basketweave, four rows in Yellow and four in Dark Blue. (See colour pages.)

- A sampler should be not only a learning experience, but also a stitch reference for future projects. It is the very best way to learn stitches.
- The Rainbow Sampler is on #12 interlock canvas using a divisible wool, in this case Persian wool. I used a No 20 needle. I have given the number of strands of Persian used on the Rainbow Sampler diagram. (You can try other wools or cottons but it will be necessary to experiment and see how many strands are needed for the stitches used. This is equivalent to doing a tension sample for knitting which, although a chore, is well worth the effort.) The spaces for the stitches need to be created before you begin to stitch. We are doing this by dividing our canvas into squares of a uniform size. The squares are created as follows:

## Tools and Equipment

| | | | |
|---|---|---|---|
| 1 | Needles | 6 | Needle magnet and threader |
| 2 | Canvas markers | 7 | Thimbles |
| 3 | Laying tool | 8 | Thimblette |
| 4 | Masking tapes | 9 | Scissors |
| 5 | Needle case | 10 | Tweezers |

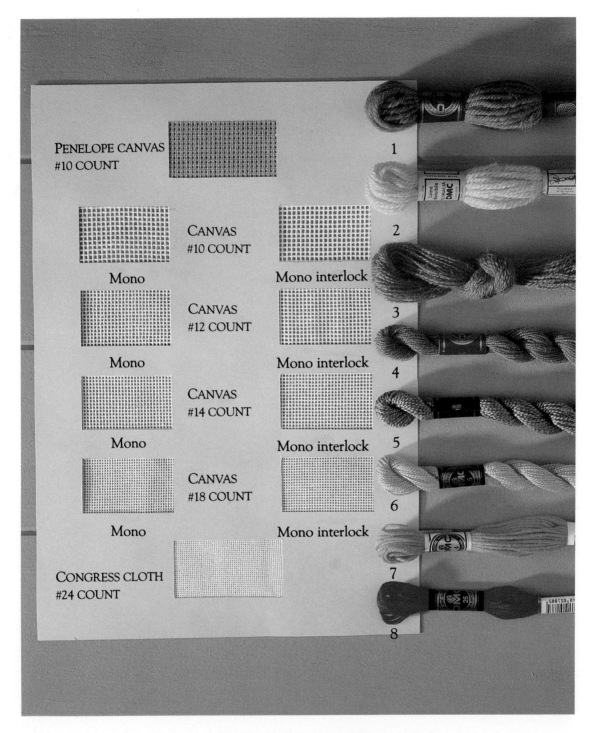

PENELOPE CANVAS
#10 COUNT

1

CANVAS
#10 COUNT

2

Mono          Mono interlock

CANVAS
#12 COUNT

3

Mono          Mono interlock

4

CANVAS
#14 COUNT

Mono          Mono interlock

5

CANVAS
#18 COUNT

6

Mono          Mono interlock

7

CONGRESS CLOTH
#24 COUNT

8

## THREADS AND CANVASES

| | | | |
|---|---|---|---|
| 1 | Tapestry wool | 5 | Pearl cotton #3 |
| 2 | DMC Floralia | 6 | Pearl cotton #5 |
| 3 | Appleton crewel wool | 7 | Broder cotton |
| 4 | DMC Medici | 8 | Stranded cotton |

RAINBOW HOUSES GLASSES CASE

PIN CUSHION DESIGN

Tulips

Petals

Boxes

Wave

BARGELLO DESIGNS

## Rainbow Colour Wheel Graph

| | | | |
|---|---|---|---|
| Yellow | ● | Blue violet | I |
| Yellow orange | Y | Blue | u |
| Orange | / | Blue green | x |
| Red orange | ○ | Green | + |
| Red | T | Yellow green | I |
| Red violet | ○ | Centre | ● |
| Violet | + | | |

RAINBOW COLOUR WHEEL

RAINBOW SAMPLER

- Start with a piece of canvas 40 cm (16") square. Bind the edges of the canvas with masking tape to prevent the wool snagging. Mark the canvas with a pencil, on the masking tape, at the top, bottom, right and left.

- Measure 5 cm (2") down and across from the righthand corner. Start with a waste knot (Stitching Hint No 13), place your first tent-continental stitch (Stitch No 33) at this point.

- Work across 140 stitches in tent-continental. Under the 140th stitch, place 139 stitches down the canvas.

- Turn the canvas 180° (upside down) and work a further 139 stitches across the canvas. Under the 139th stitch, place 138 stitches down the canvas meeting up with your first stitch.

- Turn the canvas back so the top is again in the correct position. From the right side of the tent-continental, count across and, under the 28th and 29th stitch, place the vertical gobelin-diagonal (Stitch No 7B). Continue down the canvas until the tent-continental outline is reached.

- Go back to the top again and count across 26 threads of canvas from the first gobelin-diagonal line and place the next vertical gobelin-diagonal. There will be a total of four vertical gobelin-diagonal lines down the canvas.

- After these are completed, count down the righthand tent-continental border and place the horizontal gobelin-diagonal next to stitch 28 and 29 (Stitch No 7A). Continue across the canvas until the tent-continental outline is reached.

- Go back to the righthand tent-continental and count down 26 threads of the canvas from the first horizontal gobelin-diagonal line; place the next horizontal gobelin-diagonal. There will be a total of four horizontal gobelin-diagonal lines across the canvas. Note that there will be a compensatory (see Compensatory Stitches in Appendix A, Glossary of Terms, page 109) basic tent stitch at the top and bottom of the vertical gobelin-diagonal lines and also at each end of all the horizontal gobelin-diagonal lines.

- You have now created the squares which you will fill with your sampler stitches. The diagram and the key show the stitches I have used for my sampler. The brackets following the stitch name show the stitch number as per the stitch listing.

- You will find that you need to use compensatory stitches in almost all the stitches used for the Rainbow Sampler. As referred to in Glossary of Terms (page 109), a compensatory stitch is a part stitch placed when it is not possible to complete a whole one. Always place as much of the stitch as possible, making sure you keep the sense of the pattern you're using. As you become more experienced, it becomes easier to place these stitches. Do not allow them to become a worry to you. When stitching your chosen pattern, they automatically fill the gap that is available when a whole stitch won't fit.

## Rainbow Houses Glasses Case

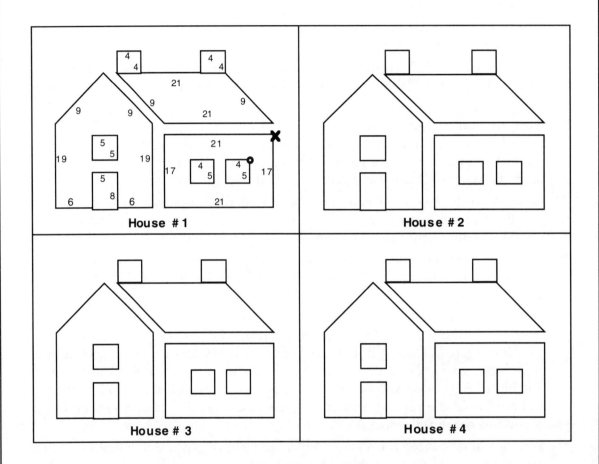

House # 1

House # 2

House # 3

House # 4

MATERIALS

- Canvas: #12 mono interlock, 25 cm (10") square
- Design size: 17 cm (6¾") square
- Needle size: No 20
- Fibre: Appleton crewel colours and number of skeins: Red 541 x 2, Green 424 x 2, Yellow 551 x 2, Violet 452 x 2.

Diagonal stitches use three strands of wool
Straight stitches use four strands of wool
Crossed stitches use three strands of wool

METHOD

- Measure down from the top right side of your canvas 4.5 cm (1¾") and across 4.5 cm (1¾") from this point. Now place the first stitch, starting with a waste knot. (See Stitching Hint No 13.)

  Each square containing a house is 46 stitches in all directions and is worked in tent-continental stitch (Stitch No 33). Place the tent-continental stitch for each house in the colour that will be used for the background.

  To place the houses, count down 23 stitches on the right side of each square. Count across two threads and place the first stitch over the third thread. This is the wall of the house.

- Using tent-continental, place the outlines of all sections of the house. Note the starting cross (x) on House No 1. The window on the side of the house starts seven stitches down from the starting cross and five across. Note the starting circle (o) on House No 1. There is a five-stitch gap between the two windows on the side wall of the house. There is a four-stitch gap between the door and the window on the front of the house. (See photograph.) Work across as per the number of stitches shown on House No 1.

  N.B. There is a two-row gap between the sides of the house and also between the sides and the roof. (See photograph.)

- **House No 1 – Red** background (tent-basketweave Stitch No 32), **Green** house (gobelin-straight over three threads of canvas, Stitch No 46) – I placed a backstitch in the green between the rows of gobelin as I thought it gave a better look – **Green** roof (Kalem Stitch No 12) **Yellow** door, windows, chimneys (outline, tent-continental Stitch No 33, inner filling Scotch Stitch No 23 in the size that fits within the outline).

- **House No 2 – Yellow** background (tent-basketweave Stitch No 32), **Violet** house (Parisian Stitch No 54), **Violet** roof (brick-horizontal Stitch No 42) **Green** door, windows, chimneys (outline, tent-continental Stitch No 33, inner filling Scotch Stitch No 23 in the size that fits within the outline).

- **House No 3 – Violet** background (tent-basketweave Stitch No 32), **Yellow** house (Algerian Stitch No 38), **Yellow** roof (mosaic Stitch No 16) **Red** door, windows, chimneys (outline, tent-continental Stitch No 33, inner filling Scotch Stitch No 23 in the size that fits within the outline).

- **House No 4 – Green** background (tent-basketweave Stitch No 32), **Red** house (cross-straight long Stitch No 66), **Red** roof (cross-straight Stitch No 65) **Violet** door, windows, chimneys (outline, tent-continental Stitch No 33, inner filling Scotch Stitch No 23 in the size that fits within the outline).

  Compensatory stitches will mostly be needed to complete the areas.

As you can see, on the colour pages, my houses have been framed for you to be able to see them clearly. However, the following instructions are necessary to turn your rainbow houses into a glasses case.

## PRESSING

An iron is very helpful in obtaining a well-finished piece of needlework but it must be used carefully. Never have the iron warmer than a 'wool' setting. Put a clean, soft towel on the ironing board and always place needlepoint face down on the towel. Place a clean pressing cloth over the wrong side of the work. Use a damp (not wet) pressing cloth with a dry iron, or a dry pressing cloth with a steam iron. Hold iron over pressing cloth, then gently press work for a few seconds and lift iron; never allow the weight of the iron to compress the stitching. When turning under canvas margins (the unworked canvas that is like a seam allowance), steam-press in this manner and you will obtain a neat edge for binding or other finishing. Remember, this steaming must be done quickly and lightly; too much steaming may alter the shape of your needlework.

## BINDING

A long-armed cross stitch (Stitch No 72) is used to finish an edge or to join two edges of canvas. It is worked with the right side(s) of the canvas exposed.

- **Instruction 1** – When finishing a single edge, fold the bare canvas so that the two threads closest to your completed work are on top. This will give you, closest to the stitching, **two** threads of canvas on the top of the fold; with the right side towards you and incorporating the completed stitching row, stitch over the top of these two threads.

- **Instruction 2** – When joining two separate edges of canvas, fold each piece so that there is one thread of bare canvas on the top of the fold. This will give you, closest to the stitching, **one** thread of canvas on the top of the fold. Bring folded edges together, wrong sides facing. Make sure that the canvas holes are aligned. Incorporating the completed stitching rows, stitch through the aligned holes and over the single thread of each piece.

## FINISHING

For glasses case, trim canvas margins to eight threads out from the work. Cut iron-on Vylene to fit the worked area. Iron onto the wrong side of the work, shiny side down. Iron will be on moderate heat. Cut lining to  fit trimmed work – allow a 1 cm (½") turning. Turn under canvas margin along top of work, exposing two canvas threads at fold as per Instruction 1. Turn under margin along  both sides and bottom of work, exposing one canvas thread at fold as per Instruction 2. Carefully steam press these folds.

Select an appropriate colour and bind with long-armed cross stitch (Stitch No 72) across the top edge of work using Instruction 1.

Trim off another three threads of canvas. With wrong sides together, pin lining in place turning under raw edges to fit. (I tacked on the lining.)  Don't forget this only comes to the edge of your actual stitching. You may attach lining a bit shorter at the bottom edge to reduce the bulk at the lower corners. Use tiny stitches to secure lining tightly and, when attaching at the top, make sure the stitches are invisible. Fold case in half lengthwise. Start at the top of the case and bind sides and lower edges together using long-armed cross stitch (Stitch No 72) and Instruction 2.

## RAINBOW COLOUR WHEEL

The front cover of *The Joy of Needlepoint* is a design by Janice St. Croix of Edgewater, Florida, USA. I first saw this design in 1987 and had always wanted to stitch it. When I decided to write this book, I wondered what would be appropriate to put on the cover. I wanted something bright that would show what could be done with simple canvas embroidery stitches. This colour wheel immediately sprang to mind. (See also colour pages.)

MATERIALS

- Canvas size : #18 mono, 35.5 cm (14") square
- Design size: 25.5 cm (10") square
- Needle size: No 22
- Fibre: DMC stranded cotton, two skeins each of Red 349, Red/Orange 900, Orange 947, Yellow/Orange 972, Yellow 727, Yellow/Green 704, Green 700, Blue/Green 991, Blue 792, Blue/Violet 208, Violet 550, Red/Violet 3350 and Dark Navy 939 for the centre.

To define the stitches I have used I shall list them from the outside to the inside. All stitches require five strands of stranded cotton except gobelin-slanted (interlock 2 x 1) which uses four strands.

1 = Milanese (Stitch No 14)
2 = Moorish (Stitch No 15)
3 = Mosaic (Stitch No 16)
4 = Gobelin-slanted (interlock 2 x 1) (Stitch No 9)
5 = Tent-basketweave (Stitch No 32)

METHOD

I have worked this design in stranded cotton on a #18 canvas, but it could be done on any size of canvas and with fibres suitable for that canvas. There are 12 petals in each layer and there are five layers. Each of the five layers uses a different stitch. I hope you will enjoy doing the colour wheel as much as I did and I do appreciate Janice St. Croix giving me permission to use her lovely design.

## PIN CUSHION DESIGN

This diagram applies for both the featured pin cushions which are shown as framed pieces. This design could also be increased in size by adding more rows of stitches to make the centrepiece for a cushion. Or, by adding even more rows, you could complete a cushion-size piece. (See colour pages.)

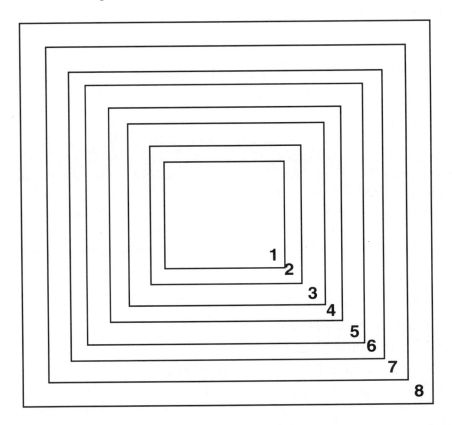

MATERIALS

For each pin cushion:

- Canvas size: #12   mono interlock cut 17 cm (6¾") square
- Design size: 11.6 cm (4.6") square.
- Needle size: No 20

Fibres for both pin cushions:

- 2 skeins Ecru DMC Medici wool
- No 3 Pearl cotton 1 skein each Yellow, Pink, Blue and Green
- No 5 Pearl cotton 1 skein each Blue and Green

The stitches used for each pin cushion are the same. The use of the fibres has been reversed. The list of the stitches used is as follows:

1 = Mary Rhodes. Each Rhodes stitch is over six mesh. (Stitch No 73)

2 = Cross-3 stitch (Stitch No 61). Covering two mesh

3 = Scotch-reverse variation (Stitch No 27)  Covering four mesh

4 = Rice (Stitch No 74). Covering two mesh

5 = Mosaic-horizontal (Stitch No 18). Each mosaic-horizontal covering two mesh – total four mesh

6 = Smyrna (Stitch No 76). Covering two mesh

7 = Scotch-reverse (Stitch No 26). Covering four mesh

8 = Rice-giant (Stitch No 75). Covering four mesh

METHOD

The pin cushion is a 56-stitch square. Find the centre of the canvas  and place the four Mary Rhodes stitches radiating from the centre. Consult the photograph in conjunction with the diagram for the further stitch placement.

## A. Pin Cushion, predominantly wool

| | STITCH | FIBRE AND NO OF STRANDS | | COLOUR |
|---|---|---|---|---|
| 1. | Mary Rhodes | Medici wool | (3) | Ecru |
| 2. | Cross-3 stitch | Pearl cotton #3 | (1) | Yellow |
| 3. | Scotch-reverse variation | Medici wool | (4) | Ecru |
| 4. | Rice | Pearl cotton #5 | (1) | Blue |
| 5. | Mosaic-horizontal | Medici wool | (4) | Ecru |
| 6. | Smyrna | Pearl cotton #5 | (1) | Green |
| 7. | Scotch-reverse | Medici wool | (4) | Ecru |
| 8. | Rice-giant | Pearl cotton #3 | (1) | Pink |

## B. Pin Cushion, predominantly Pearl cotton

| | STITCH | FIBRE AND NO OF STRANDS | | COLOUR |
|---|---|---|---|---|
| 1. | Mary Rhodes | Pearl cotton #3 | (1) | Yellow |
| 2. | Cross-3 stitch | Medici wool | (3) | Ecru |
| 3. | Scotch-reverse variation | Pearl cotton #3 | (1) | Blue |
| 4. | Rice | Medici wool | (2) | Ecru |
| 5. | Mosaic-horizontal | Pearl cotton #3 | (1) | Green |
| 6. | Smyrna | Medici wool | (2) | Ecru |
| 7. | Scotch-reverse | Pearl cotton #3 | (1) | Pink |
| 8. | Rice-giant | Medici wool | (3) | Ecru |

To finish the pin cushion, select a suitable backing material. Use long-armed cross stitch (Stitch No 72) around your stitching following Instruction 1 on Page 98. Make hem on backing material and stitch to the edge of the long-armed cross stitch, leaving a gap where you will insert your preferred filling.

CHAPTER 9

# BARGELLO

Bargello is also know as Florentine stitch and has been in use since the 17th century. It is a straight stitch worked in upward and downward steps. The pattern repeats. The most popular size for bargello stitches is over four threads of canvas. It can move up and down the canvas in as many steps as required. The steps are mostly one or two threads up or down the canvas from one another. The most popular pattern is known as the flame stitch, which forms peaks throughout the design. These peaks can vary in the number of steps and in size. Very often, they are worked in one colour with varying tones of this colour. Cushions and chair seats lend themselves well to this method of stitching. The stitches are not difficult and neither is the method of stitching. I have included four designs for you to try. Included are Bargello Stitching Hints (see page 103) which are in addition to those used for needlepoint (see page 11). Use them in conjunction with one another.

The four designs below were created to be used as glasses cases. (See colour pages.)

### PETALS

MATERIALS

- Canvas: #14 mono interlock 25 cm (10") square
- Design size: 17 cm    (6¾") square
- Needle: No 22
- Wool: 4 ply tapestry wool using four colours, two skeins of each one

### TULIPS

MATERIALS

- Canvas: #14 mono interlock 25 cm (10") square
- Design size: 17 cm    (6¾") square
- Needle: No 22
- Wool: 4 ply tapestry wool using four colours, two skeins of each one

# WAVE

MATERIALS

- Canvas: #14 mono interlock 25 cm (10") square
- Design size: 17 cm   (6¾") square
- Needle: No 22
- Wool: 4 ply tapestry wool using four colours, two skeins of each one

# BOXES

MATERIALS

- Canvas: #14 mono interlock 25 cm (10") square
- Design size: 17 cm   (6¾") square
- Needle: No 22
- Wool: 4 ply tapestry wool using three colours, two skeins of two colours, three skeins of the colour you want to use to complete the finishing of the glasses case

If a larger glasses case is required, just extend your stitching beyond the 17 cm x 17 cm (6¾" x 6¾").

The finishing of the glasses cases is exactly the same as those I have given for the Rainbow Houses (see page 97).

I hope you enjoy doing bargello. It is as difficult as the design you choose. It is a relaxing stitch to do – a good one for sitting in front of the television.

BARGELLO STITCHING HINTS
(Used in conjunction with Stitching Hints on Page 11)

a) The length of your wool should be approximately 51 cm (20"). This is longer than the length used for needlepoint.

b) Whenever possible, come up with your needle in an empty hole and go down into a hole that is already occupied. This is not always possible. Try to stitch away from your body. (Again, this is not always possible.)

c) Do not have your stitches too loose, but also do not pull them so tight that they buckle the canvas. With bargello, you have to be extra careful not to pull tightly, because the canvas will show through.

d) Another way of starting your work is known as the long-tail method. A tail of approximately 7.5 cm (3") is left on the front of your work. Commence stitching and, when there is sufficient covering on the back, re-thread the tail, take it to the back of your canvas and weave it through securely. Add small back stitches for extra security.

e) When you are using more than one colour, there's no need to finish off each time you wish to start another. Anchor the wool by taking it some distance from where you are stitching and bring it from the back to the front of your work. More than one needle can be used for convenience. When you are ready to use your anchored colour, run it through your stitching at the back of your canvas to the next area where it is to be used.

f) Work above and below your centre row to the required size. When working above your centre row, you may prefer to turn your canvas and your chart upside down.

g) In a design that goes from one side of the canvas to the other, it should be started in the centre. After placing the first stitch, the design is worked either to the right or the left. When the side of the canvas is reached, do not finish off your wool – leave it anchored. Then go back and, commencing from the centre again, work the other side. At this point you may decide that you want a few extra stitches of the design to be added on each side. As you have left the needle on the first side anchored, it can be picked up and the stitches worked to match the number of stitches you have done on the other side. When this foundation row is complete, follow the pattern that has been set up.

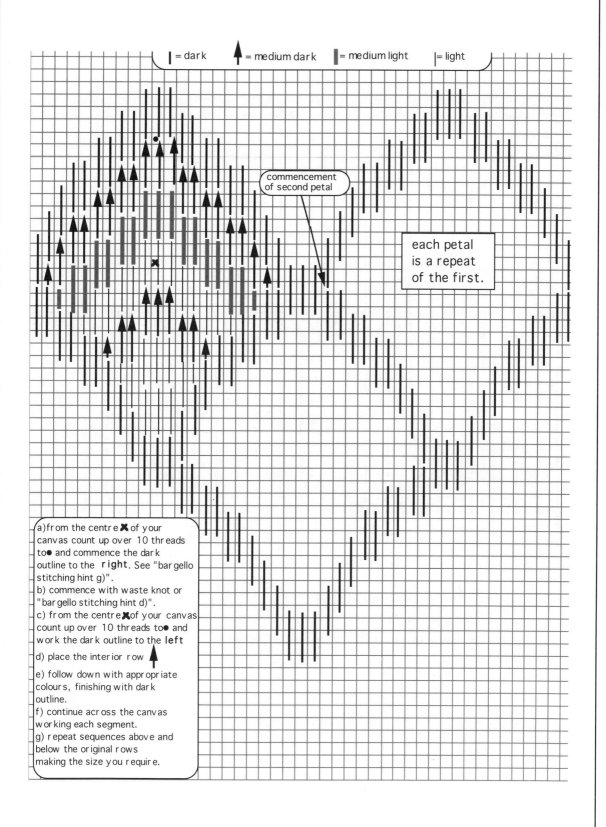

| = dark    ▲ = medium dark    ‖ = medium light    | = light

commencement
of second petal

each petal
is a repeat
of the first.

a) from the centre ✖ of your
canvas count up over 10 threads
to ● and commence the dark
outline to the **right**. See "bargello
stitching hint g)".
b) commence with waste knot or
"bargello stitching hint d)".
c) from the centre ✖ of your canvas
count up over 10 threads to ● and
work the dark outline to the **left**
d) place the interior row ▲
e) follow down with appropriate
colours, finishing with dark
outline.
f) continue across the canvas
working each segment.
g) repeat sequences above and
below the original rows
making the size you require.

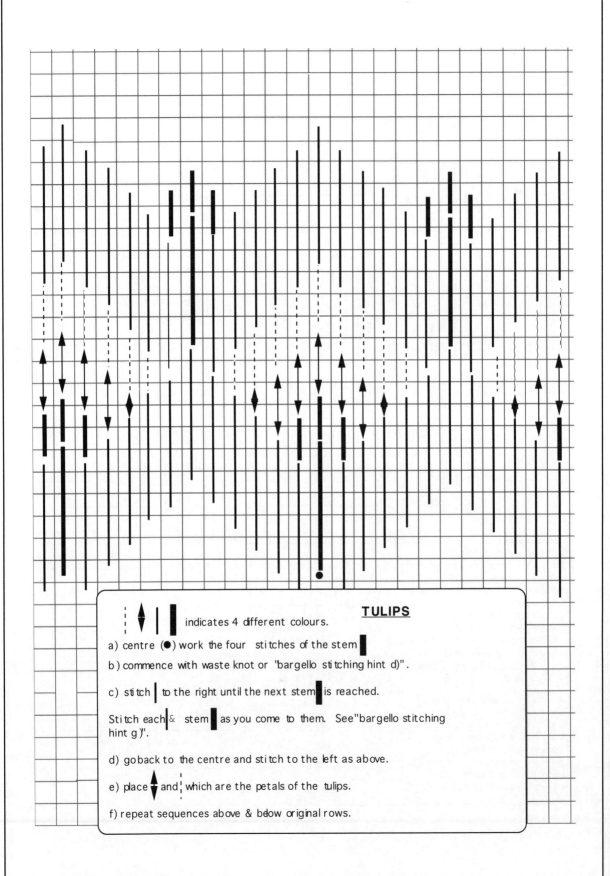

**TULIPS**

indicates 4 different colours.

a) centre (●) work the four stitches of the stem ▌

b) commence with waste knot or "bargello stitching hint d)".

c) stitch | to the right until the next stem ▌ is reached.

Stitch each | & stem ▌ as you come to them. See "bargello stitching hint g)".

d) go back to the centre and stitch to the left as above.

e) place ▼ and ┊ which are the petals of the tulips.

f) repeat sequences above & below original rows.

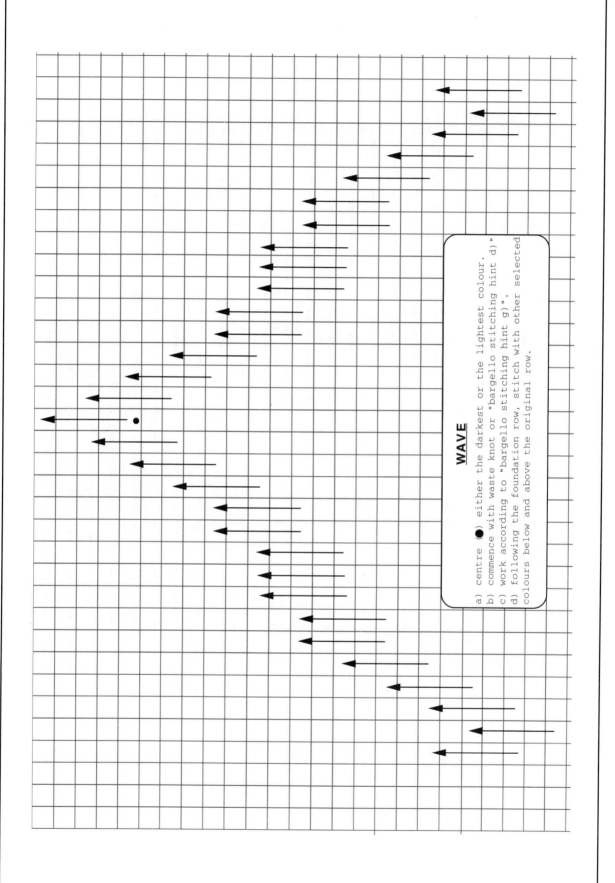

**WAVE**

a) centre (●) either the darkest or the lightest colour.
b) commence with waste knot or "bargello stitching hint d)"
c) work according to "bargello stitching hint g)".
d) following the foundation row, stitch with other selected colours below and above the original row.

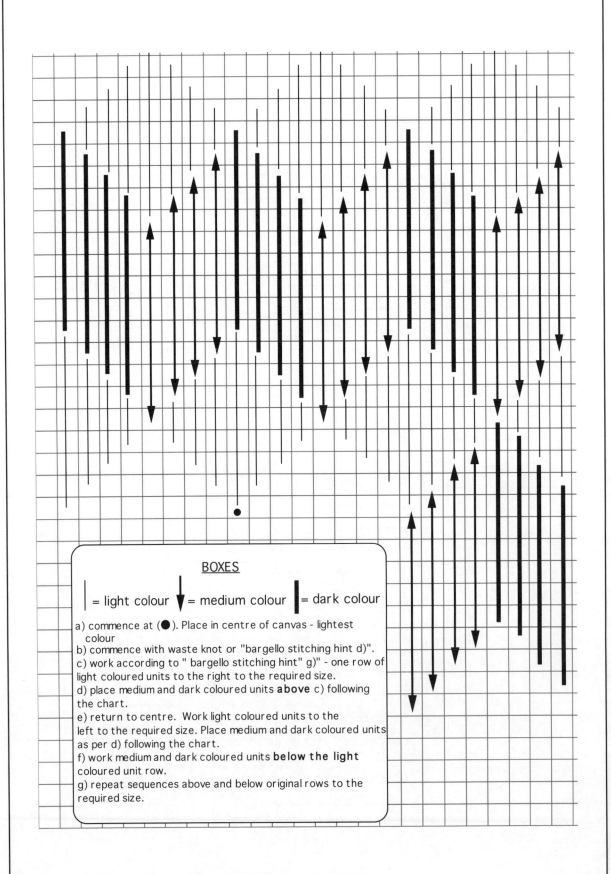

### BOXES

| = light colour  ↓ = medium colour  ▮ = dark colour

a) commence at (●). Place in centre of canvas - lightest
colour
b) commence with waste knot or "bargello stitching hint d)".
c) work according to " bargello stitching hint" g)" - one row of
light coloured units to the right to the required size.
d) place medium and dark coloured units **above** c) following
the chart.
e) return to centre. Work light coloured units to the
left to the required size. Place medium and dark coloured units
as per d) following the chart.
f) work medium and dark coloured units **below the light**
coloured unit row.
g) repeat sequences above and below original rows to the
required size.

# GLOSSARY OF TERMS

It is important for you to understand the terminology that goes with needlepoint. The following list has been compiled as a stitching stepping stone.

**Anchor**
To fix firmly.

**Anchoring working fibre**
Needle with fibre is brought up from the back of the canvas to the side of the work; the fibre is fixed firmly and can be brought into use when required.

**Bargello**
Often referred to as Florentine work. Bargello features varying patterns of parallel vertical stitches. The length of the stitch can also be varied. The 'formation' can be used for simple or more complicated designs but is always a repeat pattern.

**Blend**
Mix together. In canvas work blending colours and/or fibres.

**Blocking**
Stretching your worked piece so that the edges are at right angles to one another. There are many different ideas on how to block. The following is the method I use. The stretching is done on a suitable piece of board (I covered mine with brown paper and put a 2.5 cm (1") grid on it with a waterproof marker pen) which will accept rust-proof drawing pins, tacks or staples. I dampen my work with water, keep it right side down for flat stitches and right side up for all textured stitches. I adjust the canvas so that it lies parallel with my grid, securing it as I go. I may have to re-block after a couple of days.

**Canvas**
The ground or base material used for stitching. Mostly, it is made from cotton filaments which form holes between the woven warp and weft.

a) Penelope canvas – a double canvas with the threads woven in pairs.

b) Mono canvas – a single woven canvas in which warp and weft threads are movable.

c) Mono interlock canvas – a single woven canvas in which the warp and weft threads are locked.

**Canvas #**
When # is written before the size of a canvas eg #12, it means 'number 12'. You are working a canvas that has 12 threads to 2.5 cm (1").

**Canvas Work**
Stitches on canvas.

**Combination stitch**
A stitch which can combine diagonal, slanted, straight and crossed parts in any combination.

**Compensate**
Off-set or balance.

**Compensatory**
Adjective of the above.

**Compensatory stitches**
These can also be referred to as part stitches and are needed when it is not possible to place the complete stitch you are using in a certain area. You place as much of the stitch as possible. This then

becomes a part stitch. Compensatory stitches play an important role and will almost always be required in your work.

**Diagonal**
A line between two corners directly opposite (crossways) one another. Creates a 45° angle.

**Diagonal stitch**
Any stitch at a 45° angle. Can be over any number of mesh.

**Fibre**
A thread-like filament that gives texture or substance.

**Frame (working)**
An aid used to hold the working canvas.

**Horizontal**
Parallel to the plane of the horizon.

**Impact**
Have an effect on.

**Impact (stitch)**
The visual effect created by the fibre, size and shape of a stitch.

**Laying tool (as applied to canvas work)**
A large, blunt needle which is placed on the top of the canvas and supports and smooths the fibres as they go downwards into the canvas to make the stitch.

**Mesh**
The area where the warp and weft filaments of the canvas cross one another.

**Nap**
Soft, downy surface.

**Nap of wool**
Short, hairy fibres.

**Slanted**
In a sloping direction.

**Slanted stitch**
A stitch that slopes but is not on the diagonal, i.e. a stitch that is not at a true 45° angle.

**Skip hole**
This is a hole that is left between units of stitches. This is normally filled by a stitch from the next row.

**Snag or snagging**
Catching on a projection.

**Snag or snagging (as applied to canvas work)**
Stitches that are too long so that they catch on something. Or, fibre catching on the edge of the canvas.

**Steps (as applied to bargello)**
The number of movements of the vertical straight stitches up and down the canvas.

**Straight stitch**
A stitch that is placed only on the horizontal or vertical.

**Stranded cotton**
Comes in skeins which, for the most part, are made up of six strands. The cotton can be used as it is with all six strands, or with as many strands as required for the stitching.

**Strip**
To pull apart; to divide.

**Stripping (fibres etc.)**
Pulling fibre into separate strands. Work has a flatter appearance when strands are stripped and then put back together again for the stitching.

**Strippable**
Not a 'real' word, but very expressive when talking about fibres that can be pulled into separate strands.

**Thick**
Arranged closely; dense.

**Thickening of fibre**
Creating greater density of fibre by adding more strands.

**Threads**
Spun-out filaments of cotton, silk, wool etc.

**Threads of canvas**
The spun-out filaments of cotton found in the canvas, which form the warp and weft threads.

**Trame**
The French word which applies to the weft or horizontal threads of some materials.

**Trammed (as applied to canvas work)**
Horizontal fibres placed on the double horizontal lines of penelope canvas.

**Tramming (as applied to canvas work)**
Placing horizontal fibres along the double horizontal lines of penelope canvas.

**Vertical**
Perpendicular to the plane of the horizon.

**Warp**
The vertical threads of a woven fabric.

**Waste knot**
A knot in your working fibre which is placed on the front of your work at least 5 cm (2") ahead of your stitching. The fibre at the back is pierced as you stitch. The knot is cut off when you reach it.

**Waste tail**
A length of working fibre is left at the front of your work when you commence stitching. This working fibre must be long enough to be able to be re-threaded into your needle and taken to the back of your work to be run through existing stitches and finished off.

**Weft**
The horizontal threads of a woven fabric.

# APPENDIX B

# STITCH INDEX

Happy Stitching!

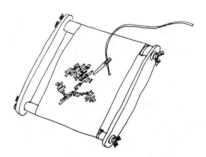